I0843243

# The archaeological impact of the late-19th and early-20th century fossil diggings in Southern England

## Bernard O'Connor

Copyright © 2013 Bernard O'Connor
All rights reserved.

Attempts have been made to locate, contact and acknowledge copyright holders of quotes and illustrations used in my work. They have all been credited within the text and in the bibliography. Much appreciation is given to those who have agreed that I include their work. Any copyright owners who are not properly identified and acknowledged, get in touch so that I may make any necessary corrections.

Small parts of this book may be reproduced in similar academic works providing due acknowledgement is given in the introduction and within the text. Any errors or suggested additions can be forwarded to me for future editions.

Bernard O'Connor - fquirk202@aol.com

ISBN: 978-1-716-17829-7

Field-walking along the foot of the Red Crag cliffs at Felixstowe on the Suffolk coast in 1842, Revd. John Henslow, professor of Mineralogy and Botany at St John's College, Cambridge, made a find of world-wide importance. It was not a never before seen archaeological artefact. It was a bed of fossils exposed following a recent landslip in the cliffs of the Pliocene Red Crag. From their shape and colour, he took them to be 'coprolites', fossilised dinosaur droppings. They were similar to those discovered by Rev. John Buckland, the Oxford professor of Botany and Dean of Westminster, in the fossilised remains of an ichthyosaurus in a landslip at Lyme Regis in 1828.

Britain had been importing guano, phosphate-rich bird droppings from the Chincha Islands in Peru, since 1838 when it was sold at £14 a ton. Ground to a powder, they were marketed as an effective fertiliser. Imported animal bones from North and South America, human bones from Italian catacombs and even mummified cats from Egyptian pyramids were imported and sold by the manure manufacturers. As animal manure, blood, soot and even ground-up rags were being used extensively on the fields to increase soil fertility, Henslow sent a sample of the Felixstowe 'coprolite' to be tested by Mr Deck, an analytical chemist at Cambridge. The analysis showed that the fossils contained a high percentage of calcium phosphate - a mineral much in demand by 19th century manure manufacturers. Being a man of the cloth, Henslow could not be seen to profit from his discovery but manure manufacturers in Ipswich did not have such moral qualms. (Rothamsted Library Archives, A1, Lawes to Henslow 13th June 1845; Henslow, J.S. Agricultural Gazette, 11th March 1848, p.180)

Within a few years, a large-scale new industry started in southeast Suffolk. It involved hundreds of men and boys digging, washing, sorting and then transporting these fossils from pits that were opened up in many of the parishes along the Deben and Orwell estuaries. It began as small scale, open-cast mining but when a similar fossil deposit was discovered in the Cambridgeshire Greensand at Burwell, a much larger operation soon got under way. Many tens of thousands of acres were turned over, which, as one might have expected, uncovered significant archaeological evidence.

Whilst some larger finds were acquired by the landowner, not all were reported in academic journals. Most smaller items were probably 'pocketed' by the diggers who sold them to dealers in antiquities in Ipswich, Woodbridge and Cambridge. Some were purchased by local academics who added them to their collections, some of which eventually found their way into local museums. Whilst their provenance may have been recorded, in many cases it was not stated that they were unearthed during the fossil diggings and often the site was not given, just the name of the parish.

Having researched the diggings across southern England, I came across a number of references to archaeological finds and this book is an attempt to document them and include relevant illustrations.

The word coprolite comes from the Greek *kopros* meaning excreta and *lithos* meaning stone. Ground to a powder, dissolved in vitriol, the then term for sulphuric acid, the resulting mixture was called superphosphate. Soluble in water, it dramatically increased plant growth, particularly root crops. With a widespread advertising campaign in the agricultural press, demand from the nation's farmers grew. It was even marketed overseas to colonists in the Empire.

Workings started in Burwell in the eastern Cambridgeshire fens in 1846. They had reached Cambridge by 1848, the Wey valley around Alton, Hampshire, in the same year, and then spread piecemeal across much of southern Cambridgeshire, reaching northern Hertfordshire by the mid-1850s, Bedfordshire by 1862, Buckinghamshire by 1869, Oxfordshire and Kent in the early-1870s and Norfolk in 1873.

More than a century of ploughing has destroyed much of the surface evidence of these diggings, but aerial photography has provided excellent evidence of the trenches in many skirtland parishes of north-eastern Cambridgeshire, particularly around Reach and Horningsea. The pits varied in depth, mostly at depths up to 20 feet (6.1m.) but in places in Suffolk, the labourers went as deep as 60 feet (18.4m.) (Tye, Walter 'The Birth of the Fertilizer Industry,' *Fisons' Journal* (1930), pp.5-7)

Given the extent of the operations, these diggings brought all sorts of fascinating objects to the surface. During the 'coprolite years', a huge number of excellent specimens of prehistoric creatures were unearthed by the diggers and sold to avid Victorian collectors. We can thank the Cambridge University professors and students of geology for the collections in such eminent repositories as the Museum of Archaeology and Anthropology, the Sedgwick Geology Museum and the Fitzwilliam Museum in Cambridge, York Museum, the Ashmolean Museum in Oxford and the British Museum in London.

At least eight dinosaurs were found amongst the fossils in the bone bed - the land dwelling megalosaurus, iguanodon, craterosaurus, dakosaurus, and dinotosaurus and the sea dwelling pliosaurus, plesiosaurus and ichthyosaurus. (Fordham, H. 'On a Collection of Fossils from the Upper Greensand, of Morden, Cambridgeshire.' *Proceedings of the Geological Association*. Vol. 4; Seeley, H. G. '*Index Aves, Ornithosauri and Reptilia*,' Catalogue (1869) p.78; Communication by Seeley, CUL. Add.7652/II.EE; Teall, J.J. 'The Potton and Wicken Phosphatic Deposits,' *Sedgwick*

*Prize Essay for 1873,* (Cambridge 1875) pp.8-10; Seeley, H.G. 'On the base of a large Lacertian Cranium from the Potton Sands, presumably Dinosaurian,' *Quart.Journ.Geol.Soc.* vol. 40, (1874) pp.690-2; Seeley, H.G. 'Notes of British Dinosaurs, part 5 Craterosaurus,' *Geol.Mag.* (1912) No.6 pp.481-84; Sedgwick Museum, Downing site, Cambridge)

This area of East Anglia was a warm, shallow sea during the Jurassic and Cretaceous periods until about 90 million years ago when a combination of asteroid impact and associated tectonic activity resulted in a mass extinction. Oxygen depletion, rising CO2 levels and a rise in sea level wiped out most land organisms and those sea creatures which depended on oxygen from the air. A huge graveyard, up to 100 miles in length, seven miles wide in places and up to six feet thick was the result. The fossil bed rested on the Gault clay and was covered in time by several hundred feet of Greensand and then chalk.

According to contemporary geological accounts, the animal remains had been washed into the sea by the rivers that had eroded the surrounding countryside during the same Wealden uplift that produced the folded landscape of Southern England. (Keeping, H. *'Fossils of Neocomian Deposits of Upware and Brickhill'*, (Cambridge 1883) pp.12-13) While washed around on the seabed, many of them  had their surface features eroded and, lying amongst the carcasses of many marine and land organisms they became steadily phosphatised. Amongst the phosphatic nodules (as the geologists preferred to call the coprolites) were found fossils of hippopotamus, rhinoceros, crocodile, whale and shark as well as those of elephant, bear, tapir, ox, horse and hyena.

Inside some of these creatures were found their fossilised stomach contents. Whilst the later 19th century geologists rejected the idea that the fossils were coprolitic, an excellent specimen of fossilised excreta has been found in Barrington, just southwest of Cambridge. (Found by Peter Blackburne-Maze in garden of Fountain House, Boot Lane, Barrington and in author's possession)

The term 'coprolites' was in widespread use by those involved in the trade well before the geologists rejected their coprolitic nature but the name stuck. Even *The Times* referred to them as *'the petrified dung of extinct reptilia.'* (*The Times*, April 16th, 1874)

East Anglia was a lot warmer millions of years ago than it is today, evidence of the northward shift of the European landmass from its position closer to the equator during Jurassic and Cretaceous times.

Whilst the bulk of the fossils brought to the surface were used in the manufacture of superphosphate, observant diggers spotted well-preserved specimens which they could sell for several shillings to the growing number of geologists and palaeontologists.

Other treasures were unearthed that fascinated the 19th century archaeologists. Many artefacts revealed by the diggings attracted the attention of members of Suffolk and Cambridge's Antiquarian Societies. These included prehistoric, Bronze Age, Iron Age, Roman, Romano-British, Anglo-Saxon and medieval artefacts which were of great interest to the many scholars who haunted the sites. Smaller items were exchanged for a drink or two at the local pub but better items were bought for a few shillings, a few pounds or, in one case, enough to purchase a public house.

With the intense interest in archaeology, anthropology, palaeontology and geology sparked off by Charles Darwin's controversial theory of evolution, fossils were much in demand by avid Victorian collectors. It was the done thing to have a collection in one's drawing room or local museum and show it to guests after dinner for them to admire with their port and cigar. (Cambridge University Library, (C.U.L.) Owen, Revd. Add.7652.I/E/74a.; Add.7652.I/E/60a., 61, 75;

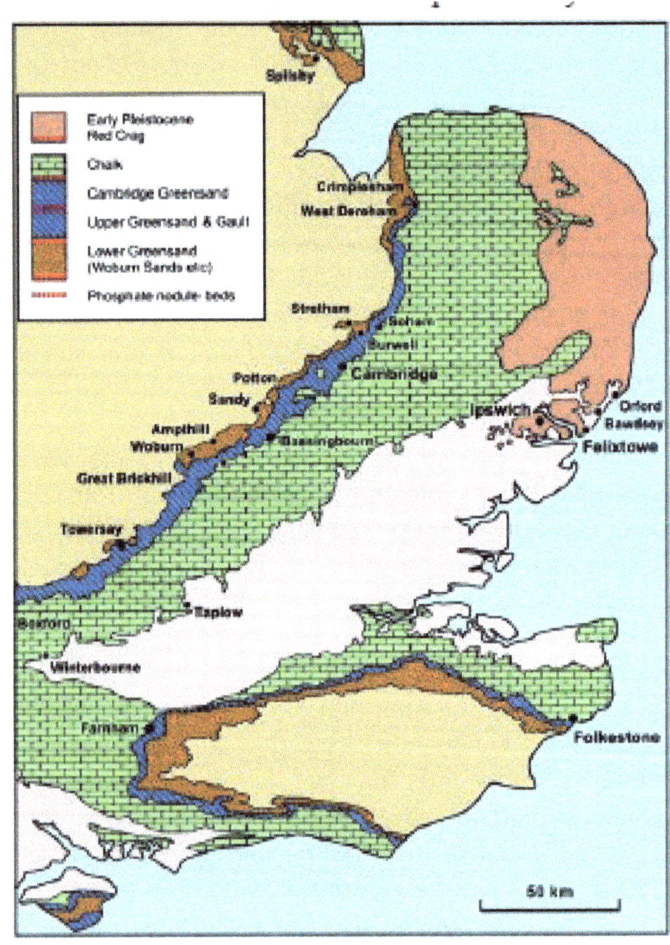



The main outcrops of the coprolite bearing beds within the Lower Greensand, Gault and Red Crag series. (Ford, T. and O'Connor, B. 'A Vanished Industry: Coprolite Mining,' *Mercian Geologist*, 2009, p.96)

The archaeological impact of the 19th and 20th century fossil diggings

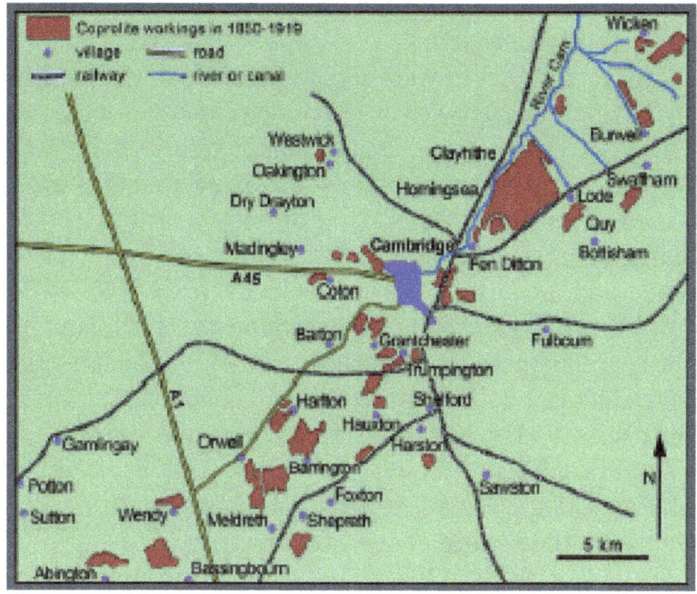



Coprolite workings around Cambridge (after map in
Grove, R. (1976), 'The Cambridgeshire Coprolite Mining
Rush, Oleander Press, Cambridge)

Add.7652II/C/4; Ashmolean Library, Oxford, Rolleston Papers, correspondence)

As a result, there were thriving fossil and antique stalls on Woodbridge, Ipswich or Cambridge market. It is quite likely that many of the archaeological treasures from the diggings changed hands there too. Given that this area's history dates back to Palaeolithic times, it was not surprising that excavating most of the fields along the extent of the Greensand uncovered much evidence from that period onwards. The industry was, according to E. Ennion, 'the most widespread upheaval since Romano-Celtic days.' (Ennion, E. *'Cambridgeshire'*, (London, 1951), p.221) The dilemma then, as now, was in their documentation.

The diggings in southeast Suffolk and Bedfordshire, where there were fewer large estates than in Cambridgeshire, were on a much smaller scale. As a result, there is not the same amount of documentation of the diggings as in Cambridgeshire, as small landowners often made informal arrangements to have the fossils raised. Larger landowners, like the Church and the Cambridge Colleges, used their land agents, surveyors and solicitors to ensure their finances were correct. Anything of interest brought up on their estates would not have gone unnoticed and some of the treasures from the diggings were 'donated' to the College museums.

Clement Francis, the Cambridge solicitor, had heard of archaeological treasures being found on some of the fenland estates that he had dealings with. When the deposit was found on Quy Fen, of which he was Lord of the Manor, he introduced a clause into his coprolite agreement with Edward Packard, an Ipswich Manure Manufacturer, that 'all gravel, coins, armour, bones, fossils, relics, antiquities and curiosities remained the property of the Lord of the Manor.'

Other landowners were quick to follow suit. (C.C.R.O. Francis Papers R89/40; Bendyshe Papers 14/1)

Not all the archaeological discoveries, however, were exploited. A landowner in Potton, Bedfordshire, is reported to have told the diggers to halt operations when they uncovered a graveyard on his estate. However, as shall be seen, many other coprolite contractors and landowners were not so particular.

It has been suggested that considerable sums of money changed hands over the numerous artefacts that were discovered and not all of them, therefore, were recorded in Antiquarian or Archaeological papers. It is entirely possible that a lot more treasures from the numerous other 'coprolite villages' ended up in private hands. A number of those documented in this book can be seen in the Ipswich Museum and the Museum of Archaeology and Anthropology in Cambridge. The latter was thanks to the work of Baron Von Hugel, who set up the Museum and who documented some of these early discoveries in the coprolite pits.

Based on my research into the East Anglian diggings, what follows is a village by village account of the archaeological discoveries in Suffolk, Cambridgeshire, Bedfordshire and Hertfordshire as recorded in archives and academic publications.

## ABINGTON PIGOTTS, CAMBS.

The coprolite workings started in Abington Pigotts in the early-1860s but it was during a revival in the early-1880s that an Iron Age/Roman settlement was excavated in the search for fossils. In March 1882 a low eminence, known as Bellus Hill, was dug. A rectangular enclosure of about 20 acres was worked, consisting of hollows and ditches of an ancient village, with closes, yards and houses, surrounded by a stockade. The owner of the land, the Rev. Graham Pigott, reported that *'Four cartloads of artefacts were removed, thought to be Roman.'* He described his findings to the Cambridge Antiquarian Society.

> *'About eight chain less than half a mile nearly north of the parish church of Abington Pigotts there is undulating ground, in fact, a slight hill trending East and West, which has been turned over during the years 1879-84 for the purpose of extracting the coprolite under it...* He observed the diggings and noted that a Roman settlement was uncovered. He called attention to holes used for domestic purposes. *'I took special note of one of them on March 9th 1882 when I was of opinion that they were receptacles for funereal urns and I find in my notes that day, 'The men employed in digging coprolite came across a hole three feet in diameter containing refuse etc. The hole went through a seam of coprolite; from the surface of the ground to the coprolite bed was 14 feet; ... The coprolite men used to take what they call a 'fall' of 4ft. at a time, and from each fall in this particular trench did I get fragments of the bowl.'* (Pigott, Rev. Graham F. 'Some account of the site of a Roman veteran's holding at Abington Pigotts, *'Proceedings of the Cambridge Antiquarian Society, (P.C.A.S.)* vol.6, (1886), pp. 309-12)

The hill was dug to a depth of 20 feet (6.1m.). Some finds included urns of a dark material which, round the middle of one and the bottom of another, the blackened colour changed to a whitish hue - the result of hot ashes being deposited in them. Fragments of Samian ware, one with rivets, a large vase with finger impressions, mortaria, colanders, and fragments of large wine vases of reddish earth were noted. Also found were four unusual circular pieces of iron, 3½ inches in diameter, and weighing between 5½lb. - 6½lb, part of a fluted bronze sword or dagger, querns, bone combs, animal bones as well as fragments of human skulls. The whole skeleton of an adult girl was found eighteen inches from the surface, thought to have been a late interment. (Ibid.) In 1884 a Roman coin of Drusus Senior, the father of Germanicus was found, struck in about 9 BC. (Fox, Cyril, *P.P.S*, vol.4, (1922-24), pp.211-233; Smith, R.A., *Archaeologia*, vol.77, (1926-7), p.186; Cambridgeshire HER 03320/E)

As well as hut sites, Iron Age pottery, Roman pewter plates, salt cellars and a scythe were discovered but the men destroyed considerable evidence of earlier settlement. (Communication by Rev. Pigotts, *P.C.A.S.* vol.6, (1886) Appendix p.cxi; Pigotts. Rev. G. *'History of Abington Pigotts and Litlington,'* 1937, p.32; Kiln, A. *'The Coprolite Industry'*, Putteridgebury College dissertation, 1979, p.47)

## ASHWELL, HERTS.

According to Alfred Sheldrick, the local historian, a commotion broke out amongst the coprolite diggers when one of the men threw out an earthenware pot from the coprolite pit and many silver coins were scattered. They were described as bearing raised designs, some showing seven stars. There was no indication of what age they were. A similar account exists for the adjoining parish of Hinxworth, Hertfordshire. (Sheldrick, A.W. *'Ashwell before 1939,'* (Ashwell, 1991), p.12)

## ASTWICK, BEDS.

Audrey Meaney, in her account of early Anglo-Saxon burial sites, described how

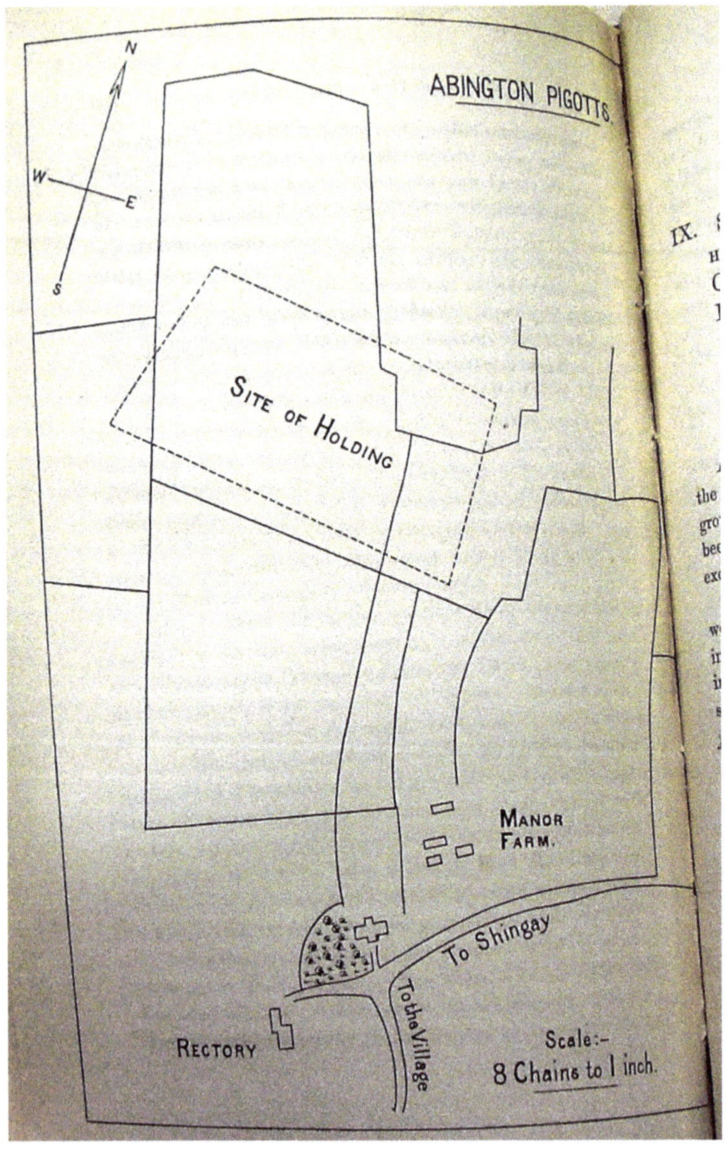


(Pigott, Rev. Graham F. 'Some account of the site of a Roman veteran's holding at Abington Pigotts, '*Proceedings of the Cambridge Antiquarian Society, (P.C.A.S.)* vol.6, (1886), pp 308)

Pots found in the Abington Pigotts coprolite diggings. (Pigott, Rev. Graham F.  'Some account of the site of a Roman veteran's holding at Abington Pigotts, '*Proceedings of the Cambridge Antiquarian Society, (P.C.A.S.)* vol.6, (1886), p.311)

*'Near Astwick a large number of human skeletons were found during coprolite digging; near them were 10 Samian vessels in near perfect condition and with the potter's name clearly visible on most of them. A sword, a shield boss, a number of spearheads and a knife were found with the skeletons. The site is on flat ground near a stream. (O.S. 216385)'* (*Transactions of Hertfordshire Natural History Society*, vol.4 (1886) p.40; Fox, C. *'Archaeology of the Cambridge Region.'* (Cambridge 1923), p.267; Meaney, A. *'Gazetteer of Early Anglo-Saxon Burial Sites,'* (London, 1964)

## BARRINGTON, CAMBS.

In October 1868, Richard Bendyshe, one of Barrington's larger landowners, leased the 371 acre Barrington Farm to Henry Sworder, the tenant farmer and Charles Roads, the Orwell coprolite contractor, for £100 per acre. The agreement included the proviso that, *'all Coins, Armour, Bones, Fossils, Relics, Antiquaries & Curiosities which shall be discovered shall be the property of the landowner.'* (C.C.R.O. Bendyshe Papers 14/1) This proved very important to Bendyshe given the amount of 'treasure' that was unearthed in the diggings.

Rev. Edward Conybeare, the vicar, kept a diary in which he recorded many of the finds made in Barrington and nearby parishes. Understandably, he began a fossil collection from the pits and, when the village museum opened in 1881, he donated numerous fine specimens along with an assortment of artefacts that were dug up during the diggings. In May, 1879 whilst investigating another case of drunkenness, he *'procured magnificent flint pestle from coprolite works.'* Bones from an Irish Elk were dug up from the Close in May as well as more hippo bones, *'but the air made him crumble to pieces,'* and after an exquisite piece of Samian ware was discovered, a *'Magnificent amphora, 3 feet high,'* was brought in from Mr Roads' diggings, which Conybeare mended. (C.C.R.O. Conybeare Diaries)

Coprolite contractors, getting many hundreds of pounds profit from each acre, cared little for archaeology and obliterated the field evidence for the evolution of the village. Cyril Fox, the Cambridgeshire archaeologist, referred to the Barrington finds.

> *'From several pits in the Barrington area archaeological remains were discovered. Between 1874 -76, North of the river, East of the Malton Orwell road and South of Trinity Farm Road, near Edic's (Edox) Hill, some 30 pagan graves were opened by Mr Wilkinson, working ahead of the diggers. They contained brooches, tools and weapons. Between 1880 - 83, in Hooper's Field, North of the village and East of Orwell Road, 114 graves were discovered by Mr Foster, part of a large pagan cemetery dating from the fifth to seventh century A.D. Again it contained brooches but as the workmen had discovered it first, many articles were never recovered. Finds from both are in the Cambridge Museum.'*
>
> Fox, C. *'Archaeology of the Cambridge Region,'* (Cambridge 1923), pp.109, 250-5).

The 114 graves were found on a southern slope to the west of the village in diggings being worked by various members of the Coote family. (Fox, op.cit. p.241) They were irregularly placed and sometimes disturbed each other. Only one had a coffin and a rectangular fosse (defensive moat) on the site containing Romano-British rubbish appeared to

Foster, W.K. 'Account of the Excavation of an Anglo-Saxon Cemetery at Barrington, Cambridge,' *P.C.A.S.*, vol.5, (1880-84), p.33

Ibid. p.35

Camb. Ant. Soc. Comm. Vol. V. N.º II.
PLATE III
1
2
Hanhart imp.
ANGLO-SAXON ANTIQUITIES.
from Barrington.

Ibid. p.37

PLATE IV
Camb. Ant. Soc. Comm. Vol. V Nº II
1
2
3
4
Hanhart imp.
ANGLO-SAXON ANTIQUITIES.
from Barrington.
del.

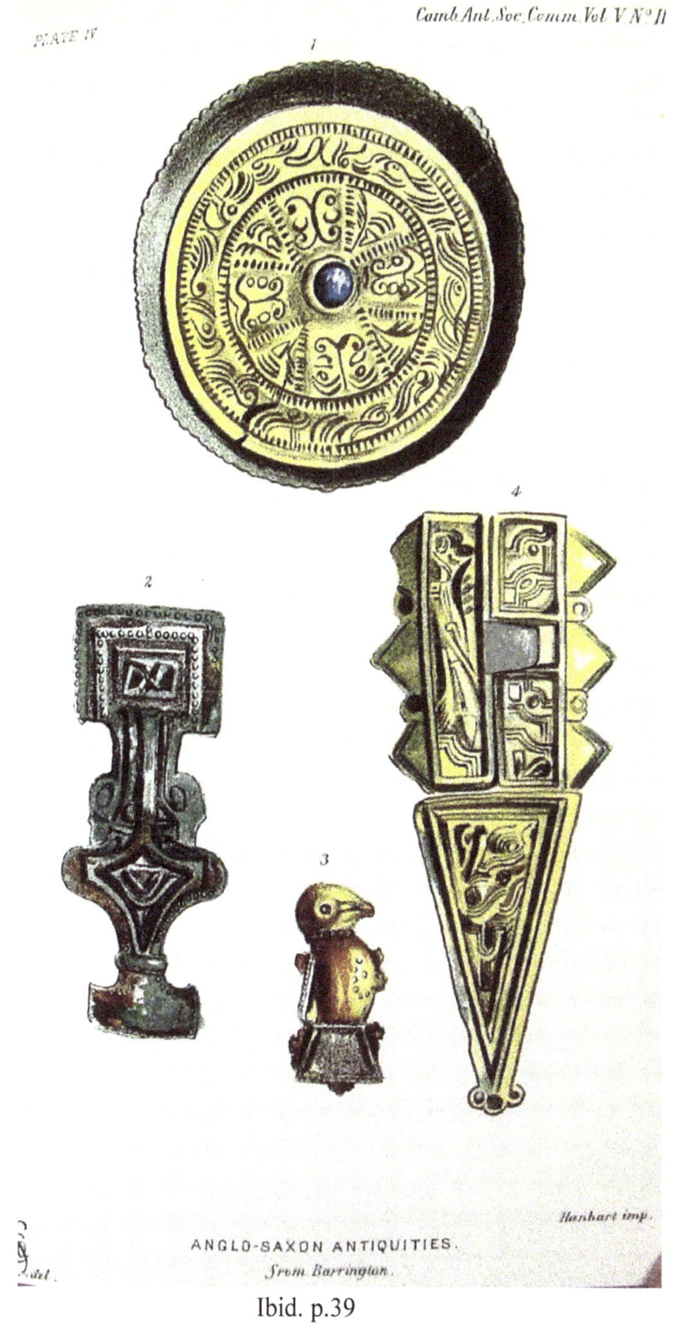

Ibid. p.39

Camb Ant Soc Comm Vol V No 11
Hanhart imp.
ANGLO-SAXON ANTIQUITIES.
from Barrington.

Ibid. p.39

Camb. Ant. Soc. Comm. Vol V N° II.
ANGLO-SAXON ANTIQUITIES.
from Barrington.
Hanhart lith.

Ibid. p.41

Camb Ant Soc Comm Vol V Nº II
ANGLO-SAXON ANTIQUITIES.
from Barrington.
(each object reduced ⅓)
Hankart imp.

Ibid. p.43

Ibid. p.45

Camb. Ant. Soc. Comm. Vol. V. Nº II.
PLATE. IX.
1
2
3
ANGLO-SAXON ANTIQUITIES.
from Barrington.
Kanhart lith.

Ibid. p.47

Camb. Ant. Soc. Comun. Vol. V. Nº II.
PLATE X
1
2 (reduced ¼)
Hanhart lith.
ANGLO-SAXON ANTIQUITIES.
from Barrington.

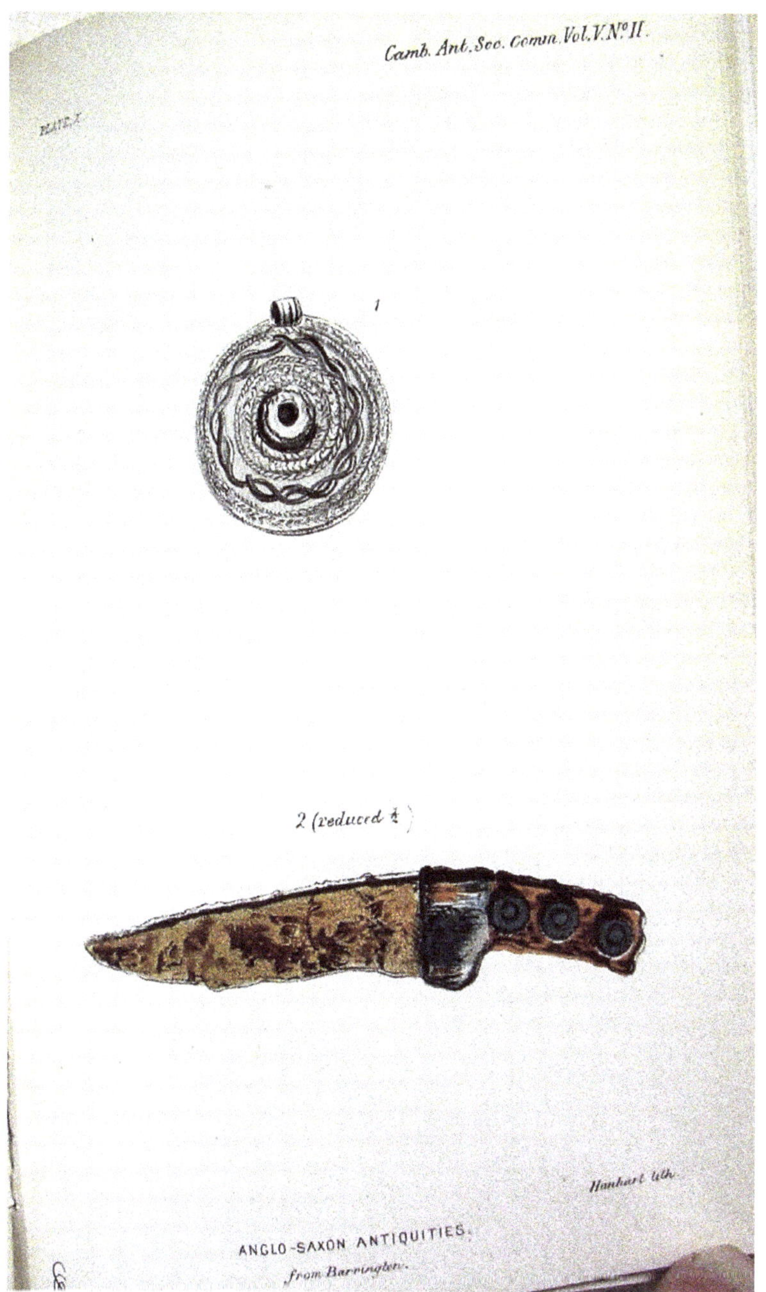

Ibid. p.49

PLATE XI.
Camb. Ant. Soc. Comm. Vol. V. N° II.
1
2
3
Hanhart lith.
ANGLO-SAXON ANTIQUITIES.
from Barrington.

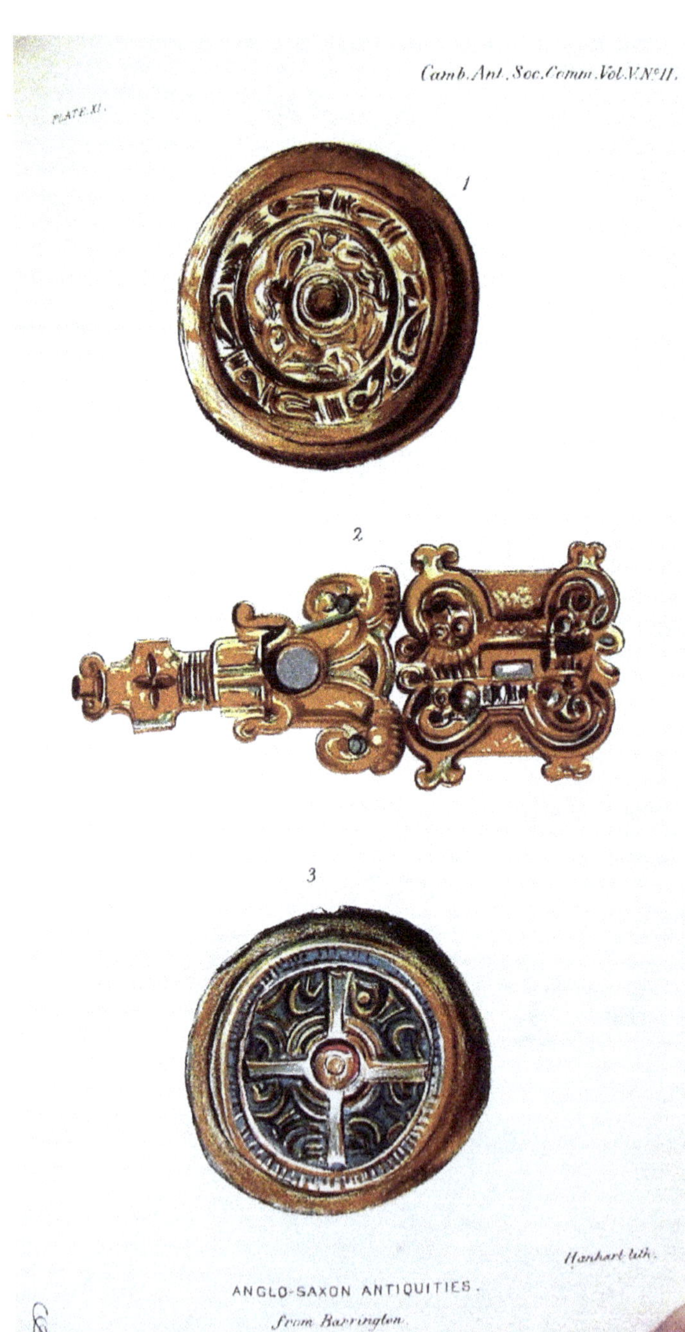

Ibid. p.51

Camb Ant Soc Comm Vol V Nº II
reduced one half
Hanhart imp
ANGLO-SAXON ANTIQUITIES.
from Barrington

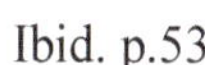

Ibid. p.53

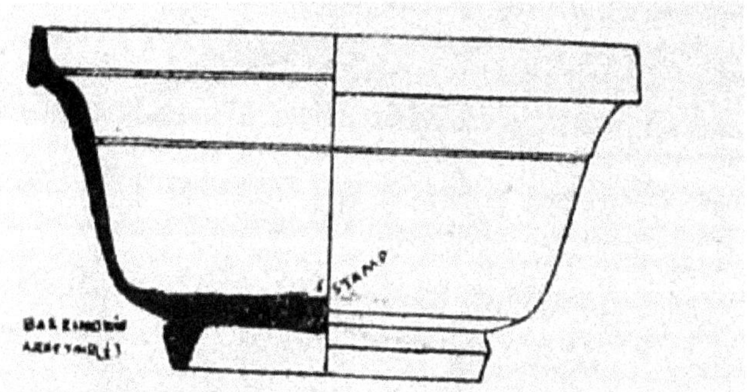

Fig. 1. Arretine cup from Barrington.

Lethbridge, O'Reilly, Leaf. *P.C.A.S.* vol.35, 1934, p.141

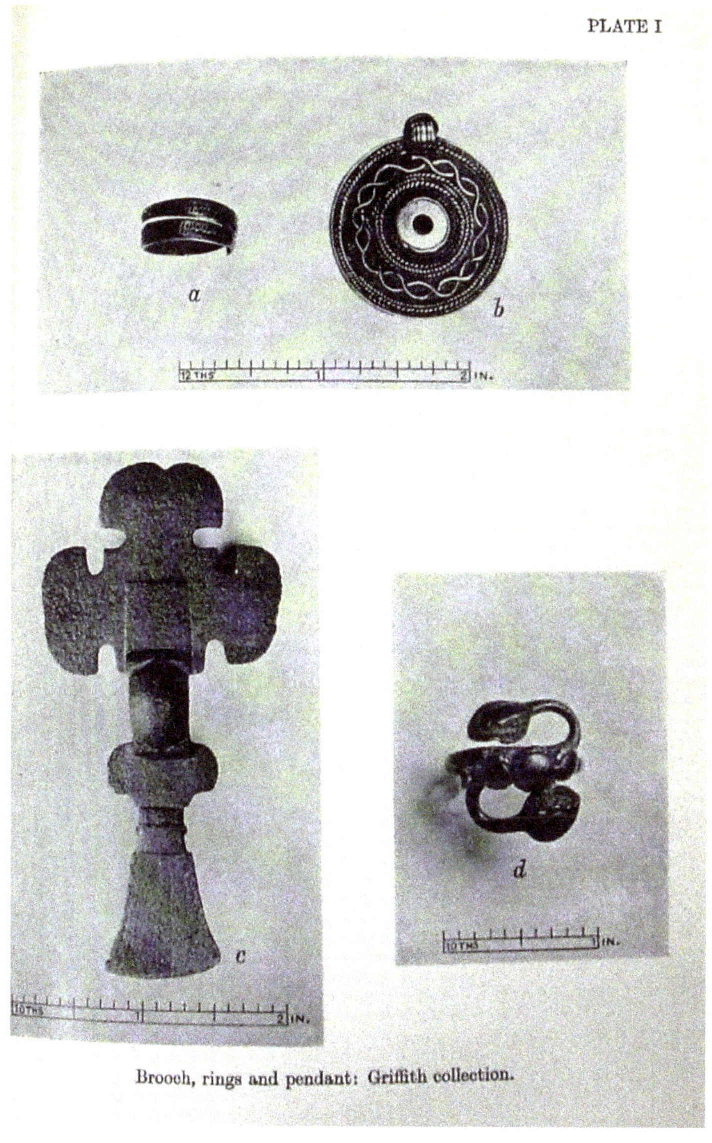


Brooch, rings and pendant: Griffith collection.

Lethbridge, O'Reilly, Leaf. *P.C.A.S.* vol.35, 1934, p.141, plate I

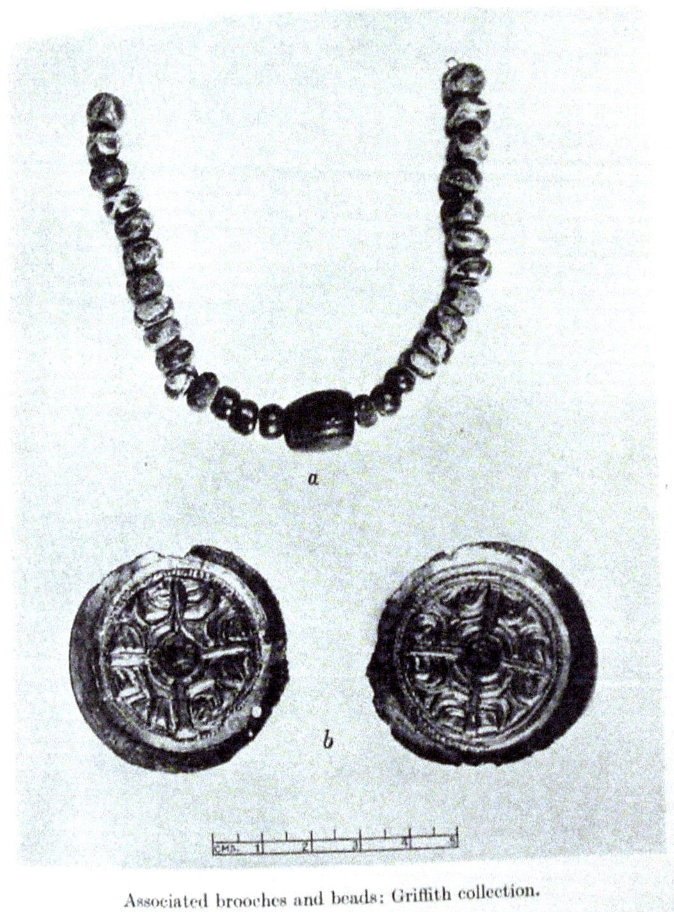



Associated brooches and beads: Griffith collection.

Lethbridge, O'Reilly, Leaf. *P.C.A.S.* vol.35, 1934, p.141, plate II

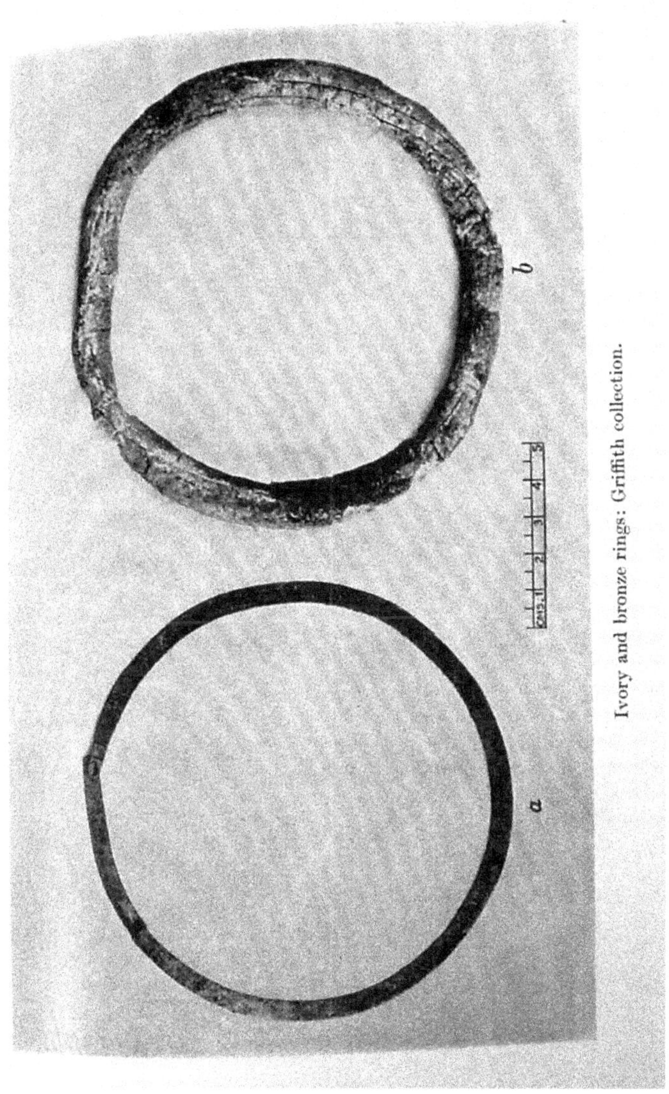



Lethbridge, O'Reilly, Leaf. *P.C.A.S.* vol.35, 1934, p.141, plate III

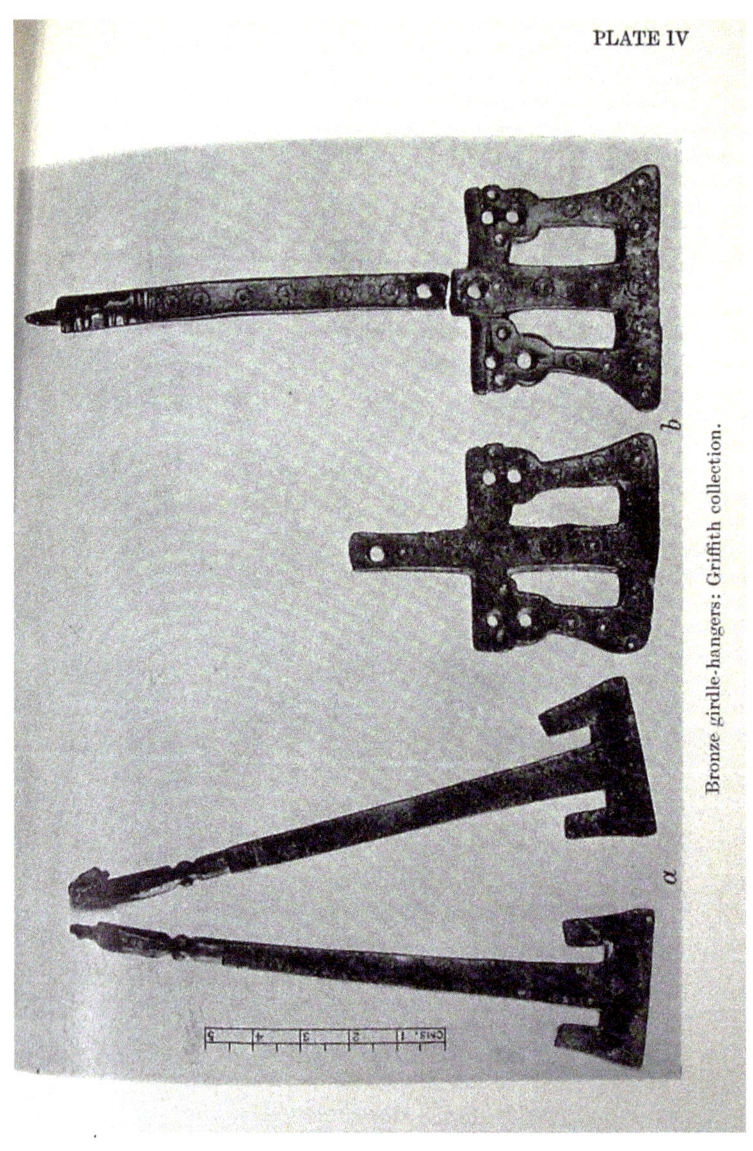



Lethbridge, O'Reilly, Leaf. *P.C.A.S.* vol.35, 1934, p.141, plate IV

PLATE V

Bronze small-long brooches: Griffith collection.

Lethbridge, O'Reilly, Leaf. *P.C.A.S.* vol.35, 1934, p.141, plate V

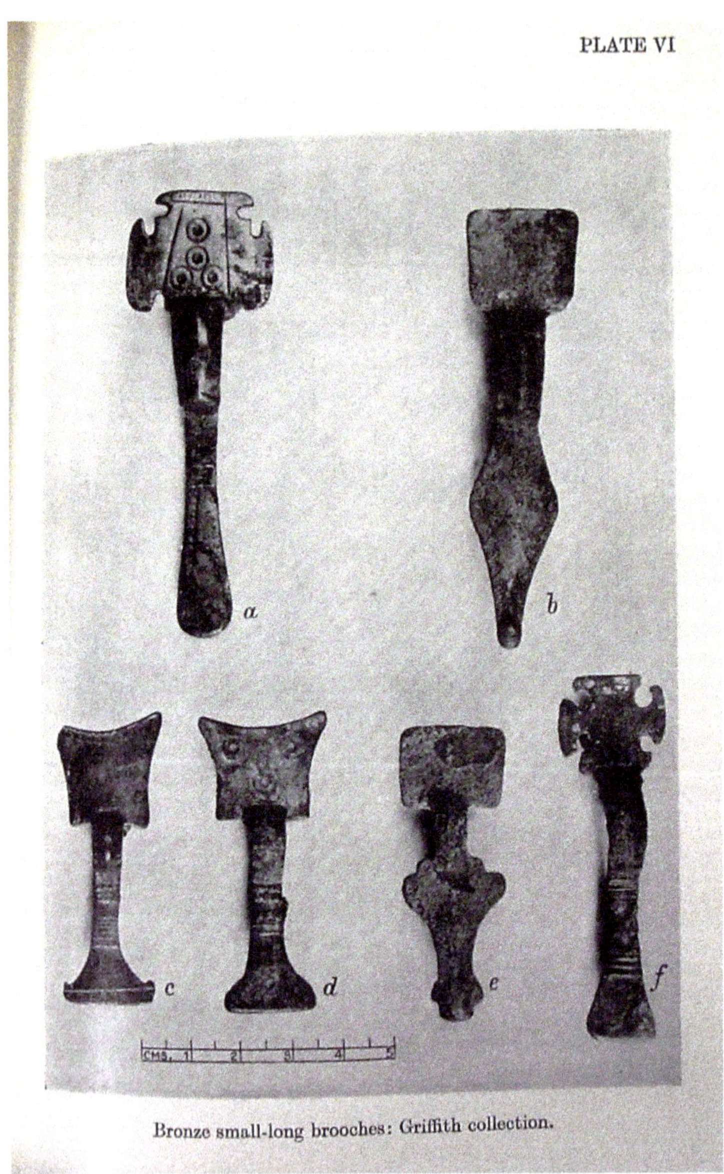

Bronze small-long brooches: Griffith collection.

Lethbridge, O'Reilly, Leaf. *P.C.A.S.* vol.35, 1934, p.141 , plate VI

Lethbridge, O'Reilly, Leaf. *P.C.A.S.* vol.35, 1934, p.141, plate VII

Lethbridge, O'Reilly, Leaf. *P.C.A.S.* vol.35, 1934, p.141, plate VIII

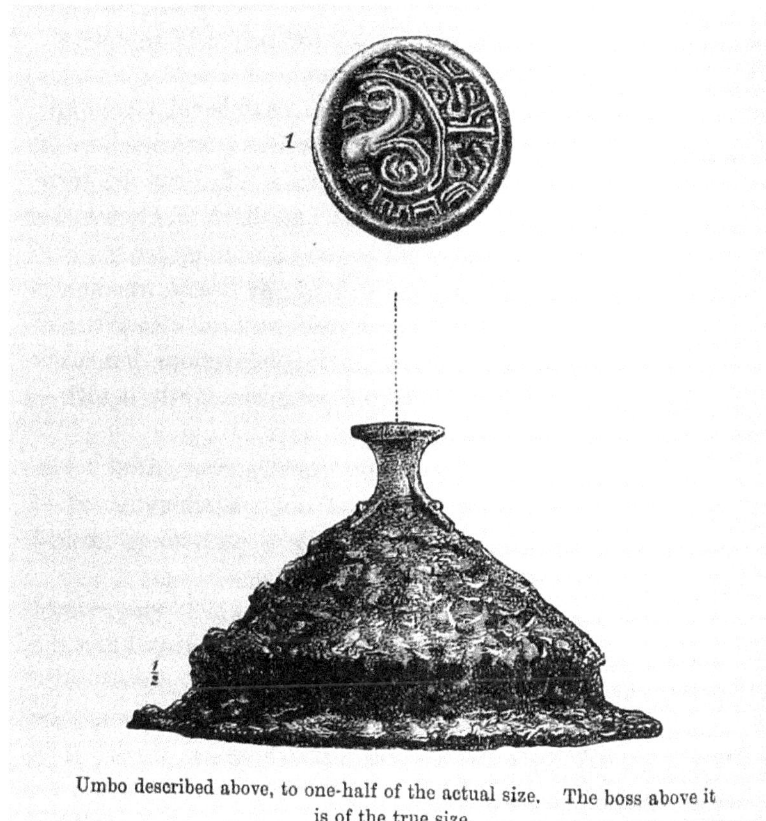

Umbo described above, to one-half of the actual size. The boss above it is of the true size.

Foster, W.K. 'Account of the Excavation of an Anglo-Saxon Cemetery at Barrington, Cambridge,' *P.C.A.S.*, vol.5, (1880-84), p.14

have been filled in before the cemetery began. Conybeare reported that *'a pendant, brooch, bead, ring, bucket hoop, girdle hanger, pottery, finger ring, coffin and an inhumation were removed'*. (C.C.R.O. Conybeare Diaries)

A number of the discoveries were 'presented' to Trinity College by Prof. McKenny-Hughes in 1879. Others were obtained by a Mr Griffiths and given to the Cambridge Museum. (Communication by Mr Griffiths, *P.C.A.S.* vol.35, 1934 ; Allen, R. *Archaeologia*, vol.56 Pt 1, (1898), pp.39-56; Lethbridge, O'Reilly, Leaf. *P.C.A.S.* vol.35, 1934, p.141; Meaney, A. *Gazetteer of early Anglo Saxon Burial Sites,'* (1964) p.61; Cambridgeshire HER 03438, 04853)

Sometime in 1880 an Iron Age settlement (O.S. TL 39244954) was revealed by the coprolite diggings which ultimately destroyed it. It was an irregular area defined by a rectilinear ditch 14 feet wide and 8 feet deep. When it was discovered, the ditch was invisible on the surface. Within the area were 50 enclosed pits, some as much as 13 feet in diameter and 8 feet deep but most were smaller and shallower. Filled with greasy earth, these pits revealed occasional sherds of pottery, bones and teeth of ox (Bos Longifrons), horse, sheep and pig. The pottery included Belgic tazzas (shallow ornamental cup or vase on a pedestal), globular urns and a pedestal urn together with imported Arretine vases of Augustan age. Fibulae of La Tene (III-IV type - late-Iron Age Celtic civilisation) were also found. (Babington C. 'On Anglo-Saxon Remains found near Barrington in Cambs.,' *P.C.A.S.*, vol.5, (1880-84), pp.7-10; Communication by Foster, W.K. *P.C.A.S.*, vol.5, (1880-84) p.xii; Foster, W.K. 'Account of the Excavation of an Anglo-Saxon Cemetery at Barrington, Cambridge,' *P.C.A.S.*, vol.5, (1880-84), pp.5-32; *V.C.H.* Cambs. vol.1, (1938) pp.295-6,300; Car, Radford *P.P.S.* vol.20 (1954) p.24; Evans, J. *'Coins of the Ancient Britons,'* (1864), p.373; *Num. Chron.* vol.8, p.155; *J.B.A.A.* vol.7, pp.122,398; Beale Poste (?) p.204,228; Fox C. op.cit. p.88; Clarke, R.R. *British Num. Journ.* vol.26 (1956) p.8; Cambridgeshire HER 03263)

Earlier items that Conybeare collected from the diggings included gold coins dating back to the time of Maximin during the Roman occupation, medieval and post-medieval ones from the reigns of Henry III, Henry VII and Henry VIII. He also reported getting *'a wonderful 18' bronze dagger still as sharp as a needle'* but did not mention from what date it was. From finds during 1880 - 81 he reported receiving:-

*'an iron axe head, Roman coins showing 22 emperors from Vespasian to Constantius, an elephant tooth, human bones, gold and silver (Henry VIII) from near Garnett House, a broadsword dug up behind Reynolds', a sword and curved knife, a glorious gilt fibula - one with pin complete from Wallis' work. ... a very pretty bronze candlestick dug up in fossil pit, a grand whistle. ... a splendid red deer horn from West Field'.* (C.C.R.O. Conybeare Diaries, 22nd March, 28th June1880, 15th December 1881)

Whilst there were considerable details of the finds in Barrington, Fox felt that many artefacts were never recovered. He argued that contractors or the diggers found it more worthwhile not to report them.

*'The majority of the cemeteries were discovered during the extensive coprolite diggings carried out in all parts of the district in the 60's 70's and 80's of the last century. Workmen went about with their pockets full of grave furniture and much came into the hands of collectors through the intermediary of dealers in Cambridge. I feel that the villages where workmen happened to reside sometimes came to be the recorded provenances of objects found in adjacent parishes.'* (Fox, op.cit. p.253)

## BARTON, CAMBS.

The only items recorded as being unearthed during the diggings in Barton were some medieval harness trappings and some 17th century trade tokens found in the workings on Barton Road. (Porter, E. *Cambridge Society of Industrial Archaeology*, Newsletter, vol.5 No.7, (June, 1973) pp.5-6)

## BASSINGBOURN, CAMBS.

In early 1887, the coprolite diggers dug over a field about three quarters of a mile to the north of the village church in which the moat and ruins of 'John O' Gaunt's House', a medieval castle, were then to be seen. This was reported to be the site of the old manor of Richmond's, part of the large dower of Queen Edith, consort of Edward the Confessor. The whole area was turned over and the moat was to a large extent filled in. The stones of the moat bridge and those from the ruins were removed and used to repair the damage done to the roads by the cartwheels of the coprolite traffic. (Victoria County History, vol.7, *Cambs*. ii, (1948), pp.15-16; Cambridgeshire HER 01776)

Being so close to the workings in the adjoining parish of Abington Pigotts there was some confusion over the origin of some of the finds. The Victoria County History reported that the Bassingbourn workings revealed pewter plates, salt cellars and a scythe of unknown origin but these were found in Abington Pigotts. (Communication by Rev. Pigotts, *P.C.A.S.*, vol. 6, (1886), Appendix CXI)

## BURWELL, CAMBS.

In January 1863, the coprolite diggers in Burwell Fen uncovered an ox's skull with a 'celt', a broken flint axe head, embedded 2¾ inches deep in the bone. (Babington, C. 'On a

Skull of Bos Primigenius associated with Flint Implements,' *P.C.A.S.*, vol.2, (1863), pp.285-6; Read by Carter, James to Cambridge Philosophical Society (May 1863); Carter, James, 'On a Skull of Bos Primigenius perforated by a Stone Celt,' *Geol.Mag.* (1874) Dec.2, Vol.1 pp.492-96) This was suggested to be of prehistoric origin. The diggers sold it to a Mr Farren who was *'actively involved in collecting fossils for the Woodwardian Museum'* in Cambridge. It can be seen on display in the Sedgwick Museum in Cambridge. Further prehistoric evidence was provided when a flint hammer was found in one of the washmills. (Babington, C. 'On a Flint Hammer, found near Burwell,' *P.C.A.S.*, vol.2, (1863), p.201) Big Mill windmill (O.S. TL 59116660) is said to have been used for coprolite grinding. (Camb.Arch. SMR 06495)

In 1867 a Bronze Age hoard was found in Hallard's Fen about one mile northeast of Reach. It consisted of 11 socketed axes, 2 chisels, 3 gouges, a hammer, 5 knives, 2 swords, a chape, 7 socketed spearheads, 6 buttons, 2 bugle shaped objects and a number of rings and other items. (Prigg, H. *Journal of the British Archaeology Association*, vol. 36, (1880), pp.56-62; Fox, C. op.cit. p.324; *V.C.H.* Cambs.i, (1938) p.279; Camb.Arch. SMR 06397)

## CAMBRIDGE

The workmen on Coldham's Common in 1857 uncovered some pewter plate with the arms of Trinity College. Ii was given to the Corporation's treasurer for safe keeping. This was eventually sold as part of the property of Harry Cross, the Corporation's Chairman. (C.C.R.O. Borough of Camb. Minutes 13th July 1857) Sometime in 1860, the diggers on the Common also unearthed a black Roman vase six and a half inches high, (16.6cm.) by 20 inches (51.2cm.) in circumference. Where that went was not recorded.

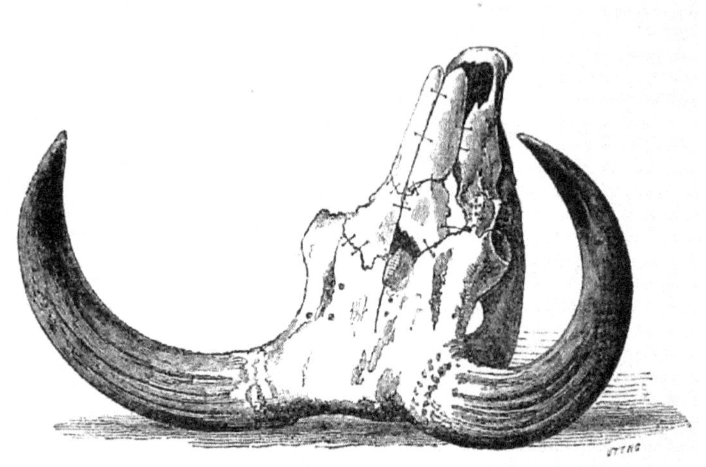

SKULL OF BOS PRIMIGENIUS WITH CELT.

Ox skull dug up at Burwell. The celt was a prehistoric axe head. Carter, James to Cambridge Philosophical Society (May 1863), *P.C.A.S.*, vol.2, (1863), p.284

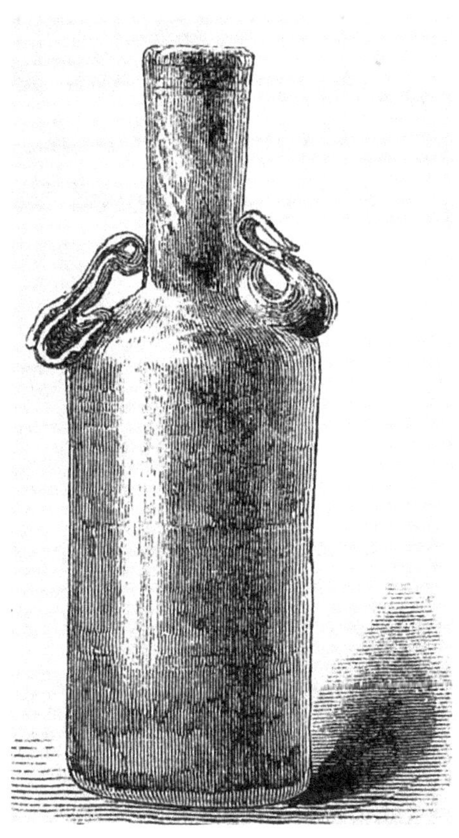

Glass bottle found during coprolite diggings  on Gravel Hill Farm, Cambridge, Babington, C. 'On Roman Interments by the side of the so called Via Devana, near Cambridge,' *P.C.A.S.*, vol. 2, (1863), p.291

Two glass bottles found on Gravel Hill Farm.

Glass bottles found during coprolite diggings  on Gravel Hill
Farm, Cambridge. ( Babington, C. 'On Roman Interments by
the side of the so called Via Devana, near  Cambridge,'
*P.C.A.S.*, vol. 2, (1863), p.293)

Vase found on Gravel Hill Farm.

Vase found during coprolite diggings  on Gravel Hill Farm, Cambridge. (Babington, C. 'On Roman Interments by the side of the so called Via Devana, near  Cambridge,' *P.C.A.S.*, vol. 2, (1863), p.293)

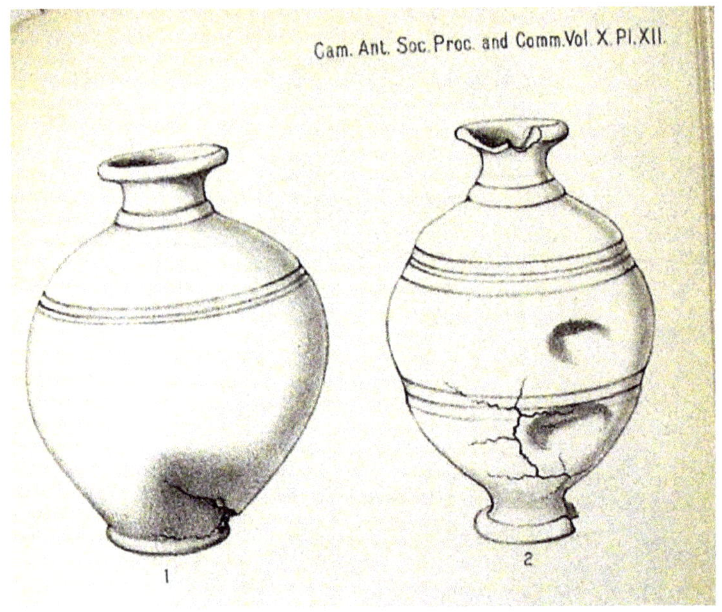



Pots found during the coprolite diggings near Jesus
Lane, Cambridge

(Communication by Griffiths, A.F. *P.C.A.S.*, (Nov.28th 1878), p.xii)

In 1861, labourers working for Swann Wallis, the coprolite contractor responsible for the diggings on Gravel Hill Farm in Chesterton, (OS TL 432601) revealed a Roman cremation with two or three vessels in perfect condition. (Babington, C. 'On Roman Interments by the side of the so called Via Devana, near Cambridge,' *P.C.A.S.*, vol. 2, (1863), pp.289-92; Cambridgeshire HER 05186) Charles Babington, the local archaeologist, described to the Cambridge Antiquarian Society other finds made by the workmen in 1863 alongside Huntingdon Road, not far from Howe House, and north of University Farm (O.S. TL 43215989). Two Barnack stone Roman coffins, placed a few feet apart, contained the skeletons of a man and woman. The grave goods included a bracelet and a pin as well as flasks of Rhenish glass, a bronze vessel, a castor-ware beaker, coarse-ware plate, a jet armlet and pins of jet and bone. These were dated to the third or early fourth century. (Ibid. Cambridgeshire HER 05129) He went on to describe further finds from Wallis' excavations later that year.

*'One of the fields bordering the Via Devana (Huntingdon Road) and also adjoining the old enclosures of Howe's Close, at about a mile from Cambridge, has recently been trenched to the depth of many feet in order to obtain the so called 'coprolites' contained in the soil. Thus many hundreds of yards of the supposed route of the Roman Road had been thoroughly examined.'* (Babington, C. *P.C.A.S.*, vol.2, (1863), pp.289-92)

In 1870, an Anglo-Saxon burial was unearthed just north of the coprolite works on Coldham's Common (O.S. TL 474587) and two ancient clasp knives. Whether the latter were from the same site is not known. (Communication by Mr Pemberton *P.C.A.S.* (May 12th 1879) p.xvii; Fox, C. op.cit. p.244-5; Cambridgeshire HER  050678) More Roman inhumations and pottery were found during the diggings in 1871 in the field opposite Storey's Alms-houses, near Castle Hill, on the present site of St. Edmund's College (O.S. TL 443594). (Cambridgeshire HER  05082; Babington, C. *'Ancient Cambridgeshire.'* (Cambridge 1883)

In about 1875 an octagonal bronze medieval seal was found in a coprolite pit near Barnwell. The impression is of a brass secretum or private seal, showing the head of St. John the Baptist on a charger. Encircling the device were the words 'Caput Baptiste'. Dated to the 14th century, it is thought to have belonged to the Knight's Hospitallers at Quy. (King, C.W. *Archaeology Journal,* vol.32, (1875) p.255; Cambridgeshire HER 04692)

Three years later, in 1878, a medieval merchant's mark was found in a coprolite pit to the north of Newmarket Road. It was made from a brass-like metal, circular in shape. *'Like all, or nearly all the seals of this period, used by secular persons, it is circular in shape, oval seals being rarely used by any save females or ecclesiastics.'* (Dutton, Reginald 'Description of a Medieval Merchants Mark and some Remarks upon Seals of the same Period,' *P.C.A.S.,* vol.4, (1879), p.187; Cambridgeshire HER 04644)


## COMBERTON, CAMBS.


Two medieval earthworks just east of Comberton village were systematically destroyed in the coprolite diggings. The first was on Jaggard's Farm, just south of Bin Brook, (O.S. TL 393582) where the work took place in 1864. The second was in the field northeast of the crossroads where the work had spread to between 1868 and 1878. (OS TL 392565) No evidence has emerged on any artefacts uncovered. (CUL. MS

[November 25, 1878.]

(Dutton, Reginald 'Description of a Medieval Merchants Mark and some Remarks upon Seals of the same Period,' *P.C.A.S.*, vol.4, (1879), p.187,194)

Griffiths, A.F.  Communication in *P.C.A.S.*, (Nov.28th 1878), p.xii

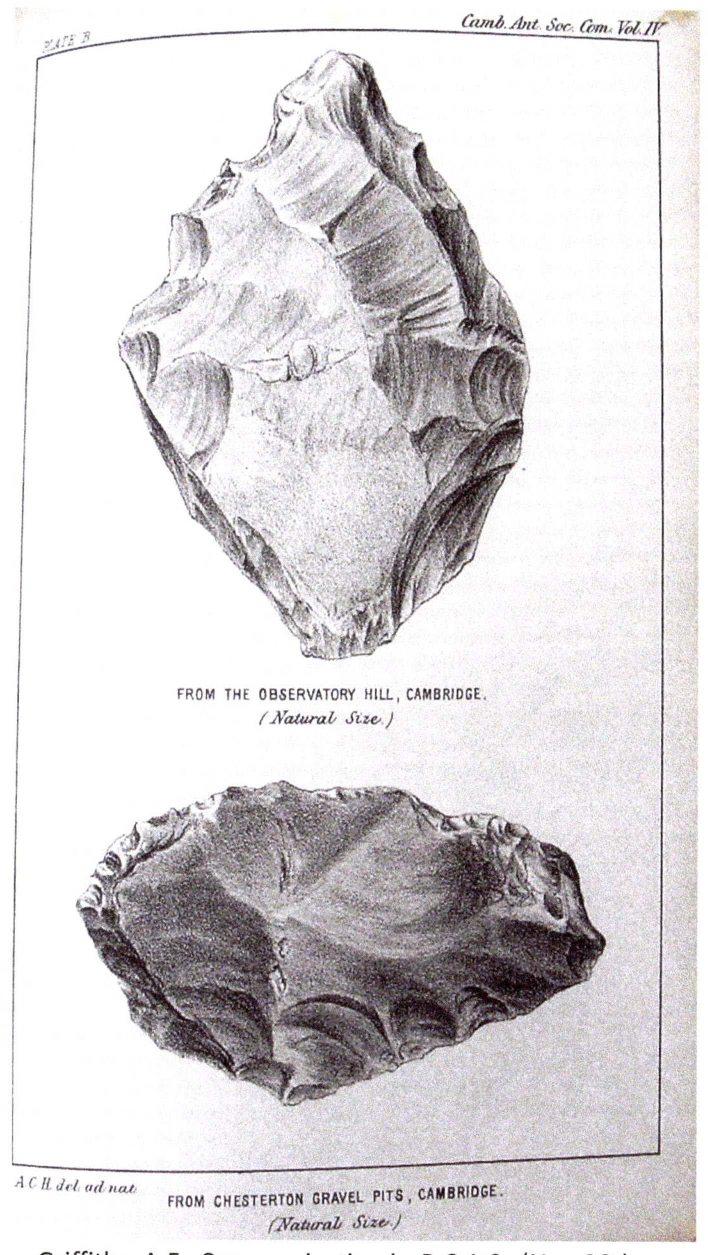


Griffiths, A.F.  Communication in *P.C.A.S.*, (Nov.28th 1878), p.xii

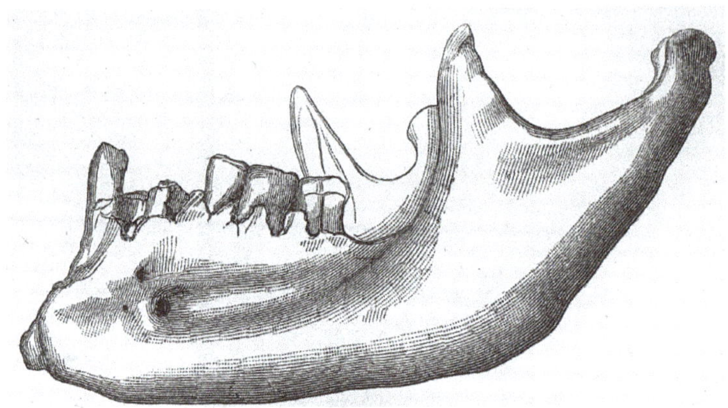

Dr Robert Collyer's drawing of the jaw found in the Fox-hall coprolite pit. (http://geology.cwru.edu/~huwig/catalog/slides/758.C.1.jpg)

Fordham, H.G. 'A Small Bronze Object found near Guilden Morden,' *P.C.A.S.*, vol.10, (1902), pp.44,373;

Plans RA2, draft enclosure map 1839-40; Cambridgeshire HER 03217)

## CROYDON, CAMBS.

The diggings in Croydon extended westwards out of the village along the slopes of the chalk hill and were reported to have damaged the earthworks of the deserted medieval village of Clopton. (O.S. 302489 - 303485)  No records of any finds have been uncovered. (*Royal Commission for Historic Monuments,* W. Cambs., (1968) p.76; Cambridgeshire HER 012161)

## FELIXSTOWE, SUFFOLK

It was in Felixstowe where the country's first coprolite workings took place in the early-1840s. The deposit was found in the Red Crag at the foot of the cliffs. There were still deposits worth extracting in 1871 in 'The Park,' not far from the church. (OS 316356) Here, according to Allan Jobson,  the local historian, *'the men in search for coprolites came upon many interesting relics of the Roman occupation of this once important settlement.'* (Jobson, A. *'In Suffolk Borders,'* (1967), pp.174-5) Few details about these interesting relics have emerged, suggesting they were sold. Some of these finds are in the British Museum and Ipswich Museum. They include a Bronze Age collared urn and an interesting circular bronze brooch disc which has a backward looking animal on it with traces of red enamel dating from Saxon times. (*Archaeologia* vol.43, (1871) p.344; V.C.H. Suffolk, vol.1, (1911) p.348; Smedley, N. & Owles, E. 'Pottery of the Early and Early Middle Bronze Age in Suffolk,'

## FOXHALL, SUFFOLK

It was in 1855 when the famous 'Foxhall Jaw' was identified in a tumbril-load of coprolite sent to Edward Packard's manure factory in Ipswich. The labourer who found it took it to the local pharmacist and swapped it for a glass of beer. It had come from Frederick Laws' coprolite diggings in a 16-feet deep coprolite pit dug into the Pliocene crag in the grounds of Foxhall Hall. (Spencer H.E.P., '*A contribution to the History of Suffolk - Lowestoft,*' undated, 118-20; Moir, J.R. '*The Antiquity of Man in East Anglia,*' C.U.P. 1927; Spencer H.E.P., 'The Foxhall Man,' *East Anglian Magazine,* April 1965; http://onlinelibrary.wiley.com/doi/10.1002/ajpa.1330070420/abstract)

*It was sold by one of the men to the local pharmacist, John Taylor, who gave it to Sir Thomas Beaver less than three months later. In March 1857, Sir Thomas passed it to Dr Robert Hanham Collyer (1814-1891) [...] who was intrigued by the discovery of a human fossil of such apparently early date. Collyer exhibited the specimen to the Ethnological Society of London in April 1863; its members seem not to have agreed on its status, George Busk regarding it as most likely from a Roman woman and Thomas Henry Huxley, who examined it at leisure the next day, agreed that it did not have the characteristics of fossilised bones from the Red Crag deposits.*

Although Collyer described the jaw as "the oldest relic of the human animal in existence" and J. Reid Moir, the geologist, reported finding 70 hand axes and signs of fire in the same 16-foot level during excavations in the early-1900s, subsequent academics dispute that it was evidence of humans 2.5 million years ago.

## FOXTON, CAMBS.

The County archaeology department Sites and Monuments record has the suggestion that coprolite digging cut into the ditches of a possible track or Roman road in Foxton. (O.S. TL 405484) Aerial photographs show the markings but there are no records of any archaeological finds being made. (Cambridgeshire HER 08629)

## GRANTCHESTER, CAMBS.

During 1917-18, when the fields on the eastern side of the Cam were being worked for coprolites, another operation was underway in Grantchester, just across the river from Byron's Pool. It was in these diggings that extensive Roman house and farm buildings were destroyed. A quern stone, fragments of mill stones of Neidermendig lava, potsherds etc. were found by the diggers. An unlined well, 29 feet deep, was excavated, the bottom of which revealed Roman potsherds, a piece of decorated wall plaster and a piece of antler pick. Charred oak beams were interpreted as part of a windlass. In the same locality, north of the confluence of the Cam and Bourn Brook, the remains of stone and timber buildings were found with a quantity of Roman bricks, many flue and roof tiles, painted plaster and opus signinum (signed works) were found. Refuse pits contained much debris. There was also a report of an Anglo Saxon bone comb. At Tartar's Well, the upper part of a Doric column made from Northamptonshire oolite was found four feet below the surface. Cyril Fox suggested that it was the remains of a Roman villa connected with extensive cropmarks on nearby Cantelupe Farm. (O.S. TL 43215500). (*Royal Commission for Historic Monuments,* W. Cambs., (1968), p.112; V.C.H. Cambs. 7, (1978) p.45; Cambridgeshire HER 04509, 05166A)

Mr and Mrs Porter, who gave a report to the Antiquarian Society about the discoveries, also mentioned that

> '*On a part of the Grantchester workings near the Barton Road and not far from the spot where local rumour has it that many men in armour were once dug up were found some medieval harness trappings of bronze, also a few tokens.*'   (Porter, N.T. 'Report on the Objects of Antiquarian Interest found in the Coprolite Diggings during 1917 and 1918,' *P.C.A.S.*, vol.22, (1921), pp. 124-5)

## GREAT SHELFORD, CAMBS.

In 1885, a number of beads, including two mother of pearl, were reported as found by coprolite diggers on Mr Gannels (sic) Farm at a depth of four feet. Of what date they were is uncertain. (Gibson, E.W.  *P.C.A.S*, vol.6, (1885), appendix LX). It has been suggested that the were found on Mr Gunnel's  Rectory Farm, close to the parish boundary with Hauxton Mill, where there were also coprolite workings. (Email communication, 22nd Nov.2011)

## GUILDEN MORDEN, CAMBS.

During 1864 - 1865, a doubled up skeleton was found with a 2½ inch long elongated and flattened bronze pig when a burial site was uncovered in the coprolite workings. The tail formed a complete ring. It was thought by Henry Fordham, a local landowner, to be Celtic in origin due to its similarity to figurines from that period but J. Foster suggested it was an Anglo Saxon bronze boar, thought to have come from a helmet. (Fordham, H.G. 'A Small Bronze Object found near Guilden Morden,' *P.C.A.S.*, vol.10, (1902), pp.44,373; Fox, C. 'The La Tene and Romano British Cemetery, Guilden Morden,' *P.C.A.S.* pp.49-63; Foster, J. *Med. Arch.* vol.21, (1977), pp.166-7; Cambridgeshire HER 02268A, 00662)

## HARDWICK, CAMBS.

In 1864 the diggings started on a medieval earthwork (O.S. TL 353582) on Harcamlow Way but there was nothing reported of any finds. (Cambridgeshire HER 03216)

## HARLTON, CAMBS.

A number of Anglo-Saxon objects, obviously from an inhumation, were presented to Trinity College in 1879 by Professor McKenny-Hughes. As there is no record of any such burial ground in the parish, it has been suggested that they were 'brought' by a coprolite digger from the diggings In the Barrington cemeteries. (Phillips, C.W. *Dark Age Index*; Fox, C. op.cit. pp.257-8; Cambridgeshire HER 03438) The Trinity College archivist reported that these and other artefacts were distributed to other museums during the first half of the 20th century. (Communication with Jonathon Smith, 25th November 2011)

## HASLINGFIELD, CAMBS.

We can thank the archaeologist, Sir Cyril Fox, for recording details of a find at Cantelupe Farm in Haslingfield where some very significant Iron Age relics were uncovered by the diggings. (Fox, C. op.cit. pp.255-9; Grove, R. *'The Cambridgeshire Coprolite Mining Rush,'* (Cambridge, 1969), p.47.) An iron sword blade, a spearhead and the point of another spear - the last found in the shoulder of a skeleton - were discovered in 1865. Nearby was a large amphora filled with burnt bones and nails. Whether these were uncovered during the diggings is uncertain. However, Fox pointed out that during the period 1872 - 1875, when the coprolites were dug north of the river, an ancient burial ground was unearthed.  This was northeast of the village and southeast of the field road to Cantelupe Farm, beside the Farm road running from Cantelupe Farm to Haslingfield, near spot height 71 (O.S. TL 413530). A considerable quantity of second century Romano-British and fifth and sixth century Anglo Saxon grave goods was recovered from the inhumations. This included brooches, wrist clasps, beads and bracelets which found their way into the British Museum, London and the Ashmolean Museum, Oxford.

Many of the finds were supplied by the somewhat illiterate Frederick Pond who had set himself up as a fossil collector. Correspondence he had with Professor Rolleston reveals an interesting side of this work.

Feb. 24th, 1874 '*I have sent you the Antiquaties mentioned in my letter to you from Harston Station they was found at Haslingfield in the feald known as Stoney Hill there is a great many skelitens beene found there was some found with those Broach but they Buried them... I have bought this little thing like a watch face.*'

March 26th '*I have got 3 Pots found in the Same Place... one the largest is figured outside very nice ... It had a lot of Bones Been preserved in it hade a Bone Combe in it with the earth.... The other 2 had not anything in them only earth 2 of them are small.*' (Rolleston recorded that the bones were human, of a girl aged about 14 and with them 2 glenoid ends of scapula of a ?calf.)

May 20th *'3 urns, the smallest very nice... They was found in Stoney Hill with the skelitons and other things. I shall want 10 shillings* (£0.50) *for the urns. I have got 4 Heads 2 are Pretty good and 2 are Broaken and some Leg Bones I have got a Bullick face with the horns on it Perfect.'*

*'Dear Sir, I have received your letter about the finding of the skeletons I am sorry I did not hear of it amounth (sic) ago as there was several found about that time but they have run the slurry over them so it is impossible to get them but I will get you some skull and leg bones as soon as there is some more found I have been and gave the men the order to get me some more as soon as they turn up I quite think there will be some as they keep finding ornaments every few days now.*
*Yours obediently,*
*Frederick Pond fossllls Collector'*

June 11th *'2 skulls and 2 leg bones and a little broken pot were received by Rolleston.'*

July 13th *'A little urn was found very deep.'*

Aug. 3rd *'A skull and some bones were taken to Pond, and sent to Rolleston. Work stopped until after harvest.'*

Sept. 30th *'2 more urns were received.*

Oct. 16th *'More relics were found in the previous week 'but I have not got any of them yet there is some Gentleman at Cambridge they give a long Price for them but I shall get all I can and send them to Mr Greenwell.'*

Oct. 28th *'I have sent you 3 urns today... the Bones in the large one was in it when it was found ... Will you please let me know if you have sent those things to Canon Greenwell which I sent in your last box ...since I have got some more things for him which I have Bought since found with the skelitons one ring was on the finger bones when found those urns was found with the skelitons they broak the Heads in getting them out.'*

Nov. 30th *'One skull and a pot containing bones was sent.'*

Dec. 28th. *'Another urn, with contents. 3 of these urns in the Ashmolean Museum still contain burnt bones; and there is a quantity of material from inhumation graves - brooches of every variety, especially small-long, wrist clasps, beads, bracelets, bucket escutcheons, etc. Several of the objects are very early in date, e.g. a window urn, an equal armed small-long brooch, a bronze-gilt belt plate with egg-and-tongue ornament; as also are several disc brooches in the Cambridge Museum. There are also, however, some late objects, including a debased square headed brooch.'* (Ashmolean Library, Oxford, Rolleston Papers; Meaney, Audrey *'Gazetteer of Early Anglo-Saxon Burial Sites,'* (London 1964), pp.66-7)

It was pointed out by Professor Rolleston that records of finds in Harlton in the Cambridge Museum and a brooch in the Ashmolean acquired in 1872 are probably from Haslingfield. As the diggers came from nearby parishes they took artefacts home and sold them. Similarly an escutcheon from a bronze bowl and a spindle whorl, obtained by Mr Evans in 1874, are supposed to be from Barton but as no pagan objects have been recorded for this parish it was assumed they were from Haslingfield.

Several years later, in 1878, Professor Hughes exhibited to the Antiquarian Society a small earthenware vessel containing an opaque glass bead, and two bronze objects of unknown origin found by the coprolite diggers in Haslingfield. The exact location was not recorded. (Hughes, Prof. communication in *P.C.A.S.*, vol.4, (Nov. 25th 1878), Appendix 7; Brown, G.B. *'Antiquities of Early England,'* vol.6, (1935) pp.785,787; *V.C.H.* Cambs. 1, (1938) pp.313-4; Phillips, C.W. *Dark Age Index*; *Proc.Soc.Ants.*series 2, pp.iii,36,77; Parker, R, *'Cam or Rhee,'* (1969), p.57; Cambridgeshire HER 04816)

## HAUXTON, CAMBS.

In 1879, coprolite diggings near Hauxton Mill revealed some Anglo-Saxon brooches and a large knobbed pot. (O.S. TL 432528) Between the 1880s and 1890s, quantities of pottery and a comb were found when Professor Hughes excavated an Iron Age settlement (O.S. TL 432526) that was uncovered by diggings northeast of Hauxton Mill. On the west side of Hauxton Road, at the approach to the mill, a Roman cemetery containing 33 bodies was found between 5ft. and 8ft. deep. Seven varieties of pottery and Roman coins of Postumus, Salonia, Constantine II were brought to light by the diggers. (Communication by Mr Kimmins, *P.C.A.S.*, Report 47, (March 7th 1887), p. cvii; Hughes, Prof. 'On some Antiquities found near Hauxton, Cambs.' *P.C.A.S.*, vol.7, (1891), p.24; Fox, op.cit. p.259)

The diggings recommenced during the First World War below the chalk pit (O.S. TL 43255284) which was subsequently filled in with waste.  Reports of a Bronze Age flat axe, a palstave and a pestle were made. (Fox, C. op.cit. p.111; Clark, J. Grahame *V.C.H.* Cambs.1, (1938), pp.267,273,288; Cambridgeshire HER 04978, 04979, 05032)

## HINXWORTH, BEDS.

According to Audrey Kiln, the local historian, Tom Hedger, one of the Hinxworth coprolite diggers, *'had the good fortune to turn up an earthenware vessel containing silver coins all imprinted with seven stars. These he sold, according to Mr Street, for a handsome profit, which enabled him to become landlord of the then vacant 'Three Horseshoes', a less arduous and far more lucrative occupation.'* (Kiln, A. *'The Coprolite Industry'*, Putteridgebury College dissertation, 1979, p.47)

## HORNINGSEA, CAMBS.

During more than 40 years of coprolite diggings in Horningsea much archaeological evidence of ancient settlement along the banks of the Cam was destroyed in the excavations but some interesting finds were recorded. The northwest third of a square ditched enclosure with rounded corners, (O.S. TL 49656214), a Roman settlement of about three acres, was destroyed when the diggers were working on the 30 foot contour. The only reported finds were a few sherds of pottery from the local Roman kilns. (*R.C.H.M.* 'NE Cambs.' (1972) pp.72-3; Cambridgeshire HER 05402)

Roman pottery was found in the 1850s in a coprolite pit east of Eye Hall Farm. (O.S. TL 503637). (Cambridgeshire HER 06372) This was thought to have come from one of the seven Roman brick ovens in the 15 acre 'Potter's Field,' southwest of the farm (O.S. TL 496634). They are thought to

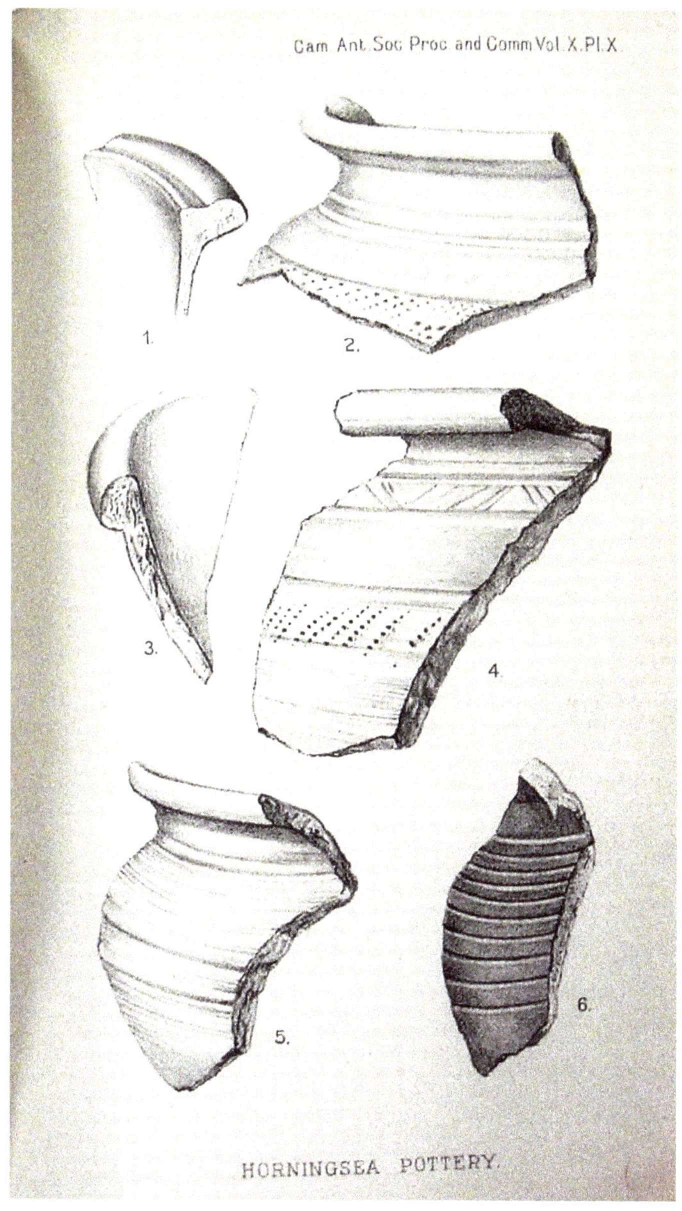



McKenny-Hughes, T. 'On the Potter's Field at Horningsea with comparative note of the Kiln and Furnaces found in the Neighbourhood,' *P,C,A,S.,* (1902), vol.10, plate X

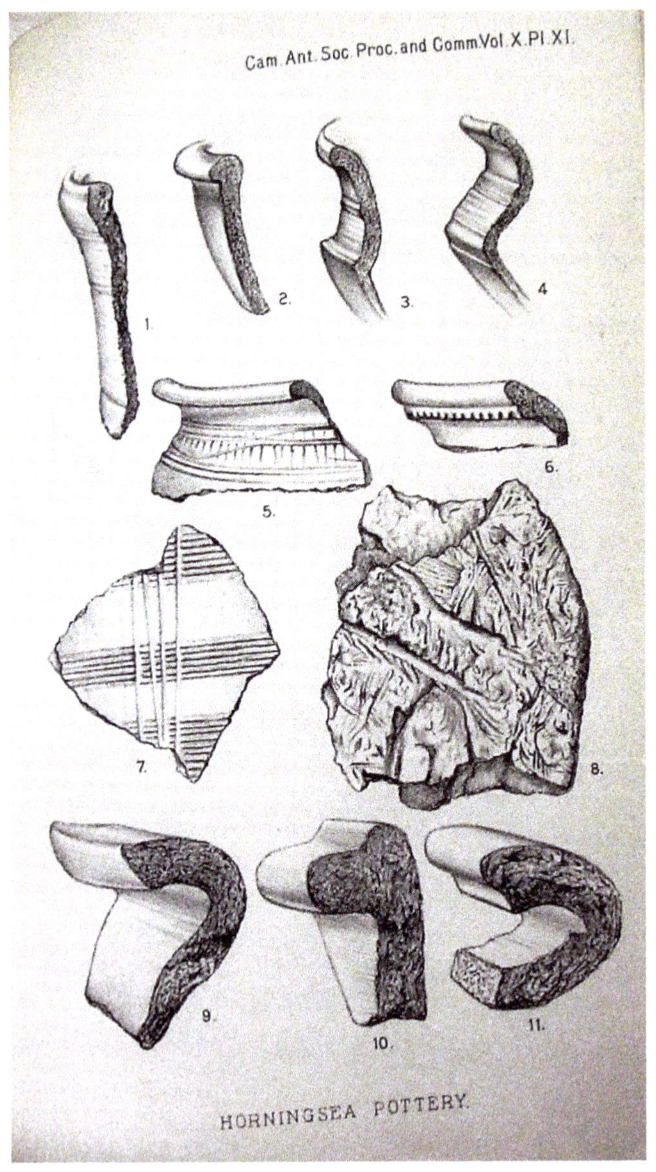



McKenny-Hughes, T. 'On the Potter's Field at Horningsea with comparative note of the Kiln and Furnaces found in the Neighbourhood,' *P,C,A,S.*, (1902), vol.10, plate XI

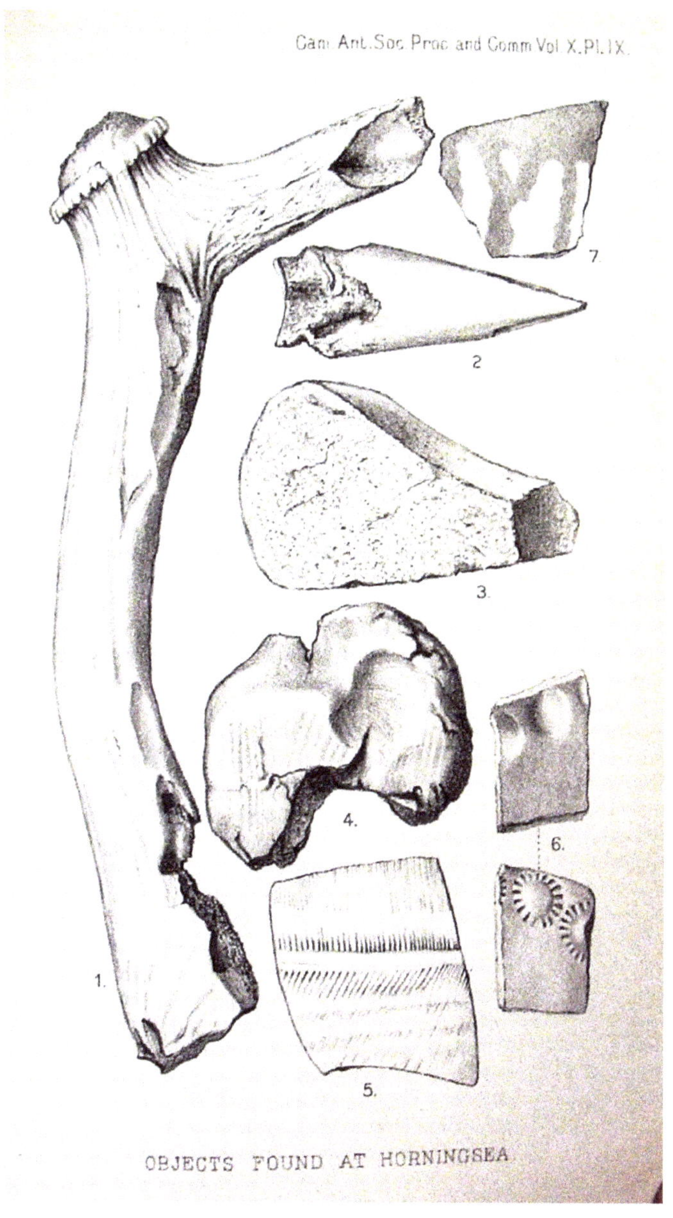


McKenny-Hughes, T. 'On the Potter's Field at Horningsea with comparative note of the Kiln and Furnaces found in the Neighbourhood,' *P,C,A,S.*, (1902), vol.10, plate IX

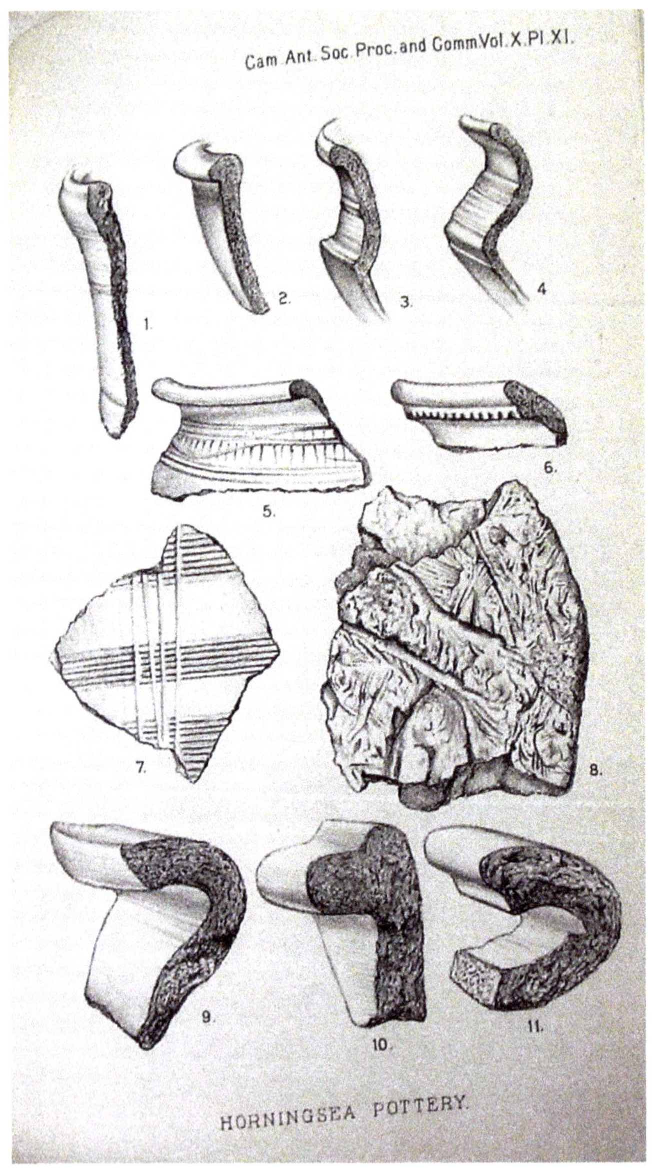



McKenny-Hughes, T. 'On the Potter's Field at Horningsea with comparative note of the Kiln and Furnaces found in the Neighbourhood,' *P,C,A,S.*, (1902), vol.10, plate XI

date from the second to the third century and pottery from the site included large grey ware storage jars up to 2 feet in height, pedestal jars, shallow bowls and indented beakers. In addition there was also some Samian ware. (Cambridgeshire HER 05546) A bronze cooking vessel and fibulae were also unearthed by the diggers which dated from Roman times. (*Cambridge Graphic*, 2nd Nov.1901,p.11; Cambs.R.O 65/04; McKenny-Hughes, T. *Arch. Journ.* vol.58 (1901) p.202; McKenny-Hughes, T. 'On the Potter's Field at Horningsea with comparative note of the Kiln and Furnaces found in the Neighbourhood,' *P,C,A,S.*, vol.10, p.174; Walker, F.G. 'Roman Pottery at Horningsea, Cambs.,' *P.C.A.S.*, vol.17 (1912-13) pp.14-69; Fox, C. op.cit. pp.210-1; Corder, P. *Arch.Journ*. vol.114, (1957), pp.10-27; Cambridgeshire HER 05393 )

## LEVINGTON, SUFFOLK.

A pottery collared urn in the British Museum is said to have come form the coprolite diggings in Levington (TM233388) but most likely it came from the workings at Felixstowe. (*Proc. Suff.Ind.Arch.* vol.29, pt.2 (1962) p.185; Suffolk Arch. SMR 03851)

## SHILLINGTON, BEDS.

Coprolite workings in Dove Close on Chibley Farm (TL 138347) revealed complex medieval and post-medieval earthworks (Beds. HER 9415) In Joan Wayne's account of Shillington's history, she referred to an 1871 newspaper cutting which recorded 19-year-old George Weedon discovering 'Treasure Trove.'

*'...whilst digging coprolites near 'The Marquis of Granby'...a workman... struck with his pick a small*

*earthenware vessel... (and) a number of coins fell out... and the men scrambled for them. The coins consist of silver pennies, of dates certainly before Edward I - possibly Stephen or Henry II. There are not less than three to four hundred... probably they were hidden away in troublous times. Applications by Trinity College, Cambridge, for restoration of the coins has been made.'* (Wayne, Joan 'A Foot In Three Daisies,' (1987), pp.64-5)

## STOW-CUM-QUY, CAMBS.

Lode Mill, near Quy, in the grounds of Anglesey Abbey, was used for grinding coprolites when the adjacent fields were worked. (Author's conversation with restoration worker who found coprolite dust in the millstone.)

## STRETHAM, CAMBS.

A mound in Middle Common, just south of Stretham, is the approximate line of a coprolite bank (O.S. TL 50767344 - 50977418). The diggings in 1877 revealed 'an old Roman burial place' where two glass bottles, two pieces of Samian ware and some Roman pewter dishes were found. (Communication to *P.C.A.S.* vol.5 (1880) p.xvi) Whether it was from the same site or not is unknown but there are records of Roman pottery found in a coprolite pit (O.S. TL 513732) to the west of the road down Middle Common Drove. (Cambridgeshire HER 06877, 06905, 06928)

## SUTTON, BEDS.

Sir John Burgoyne, the owner of a large estate in Sutton, Bedfordshire, was supposedly informed that the coprolite diggers excavating John O'Gaunt's Hill had uncovered large quantities of breastplate, weapons and armour. He stormed over and stopped any further work telling the men that they were disturbing the dead. (Author's conversation with Mr Croot, Potton, Beds.)

## SUTTON, SUFFOLK

The local trade directories of the early to mid-1880s mentioned that *'Thomas Waller occupied the Sutton Hall Estate where two urns were dug up a few years ago, which contained copper coins of the reign of Constantine.'* (Kelly's Post Office Directory, 1883; *White's Suffolk Directory*, 1885) Map evidence shows that they were unearthed in 1870. (O.S. 30624514). Archaeological records omitted the date, stating that,

*'two coin hoards were unearthed by the coprolite diggers during the diggings and they included nearly a bushel (mainly Constantian) bronze and copper coins from c.330 AD. buried in a Saxon urn. Ten of them were donated to the Ipswich Museum.'* (Suffolk County SMR.03678.)

The site uncovered by the diggers was a Roman burial ground. Some of the finds were sold and taken out of the country but others can be seen in the British Museum. One striking piece was a Samian vase over a foot high. Other finds included flue tiles, amphorae, glass scent phial, bronze pins, tweezers, mirror fibulae, gold and silver rings, a gold chain and a bronze amulet. Numerous silver and bronze coins were also uncovered which dated back to the reign of Victorianus, Constantine, Gordianus, Galienus, Arcadius, Serverus etc. Many urns were found containing inhumations, and many shells which showed the Romans' taste for sea food. They included many mussels, periwinkle and cockles as well as snails. (*Arch. Journ.* (1871) pp.28,34; *P.S.I.A.* vol.24,p.175; *Arch. Journ.* (1900) p.163; *V.C.H.* Suffolk 1, (1911), p.318)

## TRUMPINGTON, CAMBS.

Mr Pemberton's estate in Trumpington, land to the northwest of the village between the river and Trumpington Road, was extensively worked for coprolites during the early 1870s. In 1878 Mr He reported to the Antiquarian Society on a cinerary urn that was found. (Communication by Mr Pemberton, *P.C.A.S.* (May 12th 1879) p.xvii)

During the First World War, workings started again to the south of Cambridge in the grounds of Anstey Hall, Trumpington. They were known as the Hauxton Road Coprolite Works. The only recorded finds were when student volunteers in the 1917 - 1918 diggings discovered some Neolithic remains and a Roman farmstead with its own river wharf in the gravel by the river (O.S. TL 43225424). Many unused Romano-British potsherds were found on the landing place, including mortaria and ten Roman copper coins were found in the fragments. At the workings closer to Hauxton Road seven skeletons were uncovered, buried, it was suggested, at the time of the Black Death. All this area was reinstated, concrete emplacements blown up and removed and the river banks recut. The huge earth bank was levelled in the construction of the M11. (Porter, N.T. 'Report on the Objects of Antiquarian Interest found in the Coprolite Diggings during 1917 and 1918,' *P.C.A.S.*, vol.22, (1921),pp. 124-5; C.C.R.O. P79/8/27 pp.124-6; O'Connor, B. 'The End of the Big Dig Boom,' Centrepiece, *Cambridge Graduate Centre Magazine*, (Michaelmas 1991) pp.8-10; Cambridgeshire HER 04929)

## WICKEN, CAMBS.

The coprolite diggings  in 1877 revealed three sepulchral urns, found together with a small one, *'on the east side of the old West River in the parish of Wicken, opposite to Dimmock's Cote in the parish of Stretham.'* It was suggested that they were Roman as there was an *'old Roman burial place'* a mile away in Stretham. (Communication to *P.C.A.S.* vol.5 (1880) p.xv)

Bibliography

Books and Journals
Allen, R. *Archaeologia*, vol.56 Pt 1, (1898), pp.39-56
Anonymous communication, *J.B.A.A.* vol.7, pp.122,398
Anonymous communication, *P.C.A.S.* vol.5 (1880) p.xv
Anonymous communication, *P.C.A.S.* vol.5 (1880) p.xvi
Anonymous communication, *P.C.A.S.*, vol.5, (1880-84), pp.7-10
Anonymous communication, *Proc.Soc.Ants.* series 2, pp.iii,36,77
Anonymous communication, *Proc.Suff.Ind.Arch.* vol.30 (1965), p.2
*Archaeologia* vol.43, (1871) p.344
*Arch. Journ.* (1871) pp.28,34
*Arch. Journ.* (1900) p.163
Babington, C. 'On a Flint Hammer, found near Burwell,' *P.C.A.S.*, vol.2, (1863), p.201
Babington, C. 'On Roman Interments by the side of the so called Via Devana, near Cambridge,' *P.C.A.S.*, vol. 2, (1863), pp.289-92
Babington, C. '*Ancient Cambridgeshire*,' Cambridge 1883
Babington C. 'On Anglo-Saxon Remains found near Barrington in Cambs.,' *P.C.A.S.*, vol.5, (1880-84), pp.7-10; Beale Poste p.204,228
Brown, G.B. '*Antiquities of Early England*,' vol.6, (1935) pp.785,787
Car, Radford *P.P.S.* vol.20 (1954) p.24
Carter, James to Cambridge Philosophical Society (May 1863), *P.C.A.S.*, vol.2, (1863), pp.285-6
Carter, James, 'On a Skull of Bos Primigenius perforated by a Stone Celt,' *Geol.Mag.* (1874) Dec.2, Vol.1 pp.492-96
Clark, J. Grahame, *V.C.H.* Cambs.1, (1938), pp.267,273, 288
Clarke, R.R. *British Num. Journ.* vol.26 (1956) p.8
Corder, P. *Arch.Journ.* vol.114, (1957), pp.10-27

Cremo, M. and Thompson, R. *The Hidden History of the Human Race*, Bhaktivedanta Book Publishing, 1996

Dutton, Reginald 'Description of a Medieval Merchants Mark and some Remarks upon Seals of the same Period,' *P.C.A.S.*, vol.4, (1879), p.187

Ennion, E. *'Cambridgeshire'* , (London, 1951), p.221

Evans, J. *'Coins of the Ancient Britons,'* (1864), p.373

Fordham, H. 'On a Collection of Fossils from the Upper Greensand, of Morden, Cambridgeshire.' *Proceedings of the Geological Association*. Vol. 4

Fordham, H.G. 'A Small Bronze Object found near Guilden Morden,' *P.C.A.S.*, vol.10, (1902), pp.44,373

Foster, W.K. 'Account of the Excavation of an Anglo-Saxon Cemetery at Barrington, Cambridge,' *P.C.A.S.*, vol.5, (1880-84), pp.xii, 5-32

Gibson, E.W. *P.C.A.S*, vol.6, (1885), appendix LX

Grove, R. *'The Cambridgeshire Coprolite Mining Rush,'* (Cambridge, 1969), p.47

Fox, C. and Lethbridge, T. 'The La Tene and Romano British Cemetery, Guilden Morden,' *P.C.A.S.* (1926), pp.49-63

Foster, J. *Med. Arch.* vol.21, (1977), pp.166-7

Fox, Cyril, *P.P.S*, vol.4, (1922-24), pp.211-233

Fox, C. 'The *Archaeology of the Cambridge Region.'* (Cambridge 1923), pp.88, 109, 111, 210-1, 244-5, 250-9, 267, 324

Griffiths, A.F. Communication in *P.C.A.S.*, (Nov.28th 1878), p.xii

Griffiths, Communication in *P.C.A.S.* vol.35, 1934

Grove, R. *'The Cambridgeshire Coprolite Mining Rush'*, (Cambridge 1969)

Hughes, Prof. Communication in *P.C.A.S.*, vol.4, (Nov. 25th 1878), Appendix 7

Hughes, Prof. 'On some Antiquities found near Hauxton, Cambs.' *P.C.A.S.*, vol.7, (1891), p.24

Keeping, H. '*Fossils of Neocomian Deposits of Upware and Brickhill*', (Cambridge 1883) pp.12-13
*Kelly's Post Office Directory*, Suffolk, Sutton, 1883
Kiln, A. '*The Coprolite Industry*', Putteridgebury College dissertation, 1979, p.47
Kimmins, Communication in *P.C.A.S.*, Report 47, (March 7th 1887), p. cvii
Jobson, A. '*In Suffolk Borders,*' (1967), pp.174-5
Kiln, A. '*The Coprolite Industry*', Putteridgebury College dissertation, 1979, p.47
King, C.W. *Archaeology Journal,* vol.32, (1875) p.255
Lethbridge, O'Reilly, Leaf. *P.C.A.S.* vol.35, 1934, p.141
Lucas, C. '*The Fenman's World,*' (Norwich 1930), pp.25-32
McKenny-Hughes, T. *Arch. Journ.* vol.58 (1901) p.202
McKenny-Hughes, T. 'On the Potter's Field at Horningsea with comparative note of the Kiln and Furnaces found in the Neighbourhood,' *P,C,A,S.*, vol.10, p.174
Meaney, A. '*Gazetteer of Early Anglo-Saxon Burial Sites,*' (London, 1964) p.61, 66-7
*Num. Chron.* vol.8, p.155
Moir, J.R. '*The Antiquity of Man in East Anglia,*' C.U.P., 1927
O'Connor, B. 'The End of the Big Dig Boom,' Centrepiece, *Cambridge Graduate Centre Magazine*, (Michaelmas 1991) pp.8-10
Parker, R, '*Cam or Rhee,*' (1969), p.57
Pemberton, Communication in *P.C.A.S.* (May 12th 1879) p.xvii
Phillips, C.W. *Dark Age Index*
Pigott, Rev. Graham F. 'Some account of the site of a Roman veteran's holding at Abington Pigotts, '*Proceedings*

*of the Cambridge Antiquarian Society, (P.C.A.S.)* vol.6, (1886), pp. 309-12

Pigotts, Rev. *P.* Communication in *P.C.A.S.* vol.6, (1886), Appendix p.cxi

Pigotts. Rev. G. '*History of Abington Pigotts and Litlington,'* 1937, p.32

Porter, N.T. 'Report on the Objects of Antiquarian Interest found in the Coprolite Diggings during 1917 and 1918,' *P.C.A.S.*, vol.22, (1921), pp. 124-5

Porter, E. *Cambridge Society of Industrial Archaeology,* Newsletter, vol.5 No.7, (June, 1973) pp.5-6

Prigg, H. *Journal of the British Archaeology Association*, vol. 36, (1880), pp.56-62

*Proc. Suff.Ind.Arch.* vol.24,p.175

*Proc. Suff.Ind.Arch.* vol.29, pt.2 (1962) p.185

Seeley, H. G. '*Index Aves, Ornithosauri and Reptilia,'* Catalogue (1869) p.78; Communication by Seeley, CUL. Add.7652/II.EE

Teall, J.J. 'The Potton and Wicken Phosphatic Deposits,' *Sedgwick Prize Essay for 1873,* (Cambridge 1875) pp.8-10; Seeley, H.G. 'On the base of a large Lacertian Cranium from the Potton Sands, presumably Dinosaurian,' *Quart.Journ.Geol.Soc.* vol. 40, (1874) pp.690-2

*Royal Commission for Historic Monuments,* 'W. Cambs.' , (1968) p.76, 112

*Royal Commission for Historic Monuments,* 'NE Cambs.' , (1972) pp.72-3

Seeley, H.G. 'Notes of British Dinosaurs, part 5 Craterosaurus,' *Geol.Mag.* (1912) No.6 pp.481-84

Sheldrick, A.W. '*Ashwell before 1939,*'   (Ashwell, 1991), p.12
Smedley, N. & Owles, E. 'Pottery of the Early and Early Middle Bronze Age in Suffolk,' *Proc.Suff.Ind.Arch.* vol. 29, pt.2 (1962) p.185
Smith, R.A., *Archaeologia*, vol.77, (1926-7), p.186
Spencer H.E.P., '*A contribution to the History of Suffolk - Lowestoft,*'   undated, 118-20
Spencer H.E.P., 'The Foxhall Man,' *East Anglian Magazine*, April 1965
*Transactions of Hertfordshire Natural History Society*, vol.4 (1886) p.40
Tye, Walter 'The Birth of the Fertilizer Industry,' *Fisons' Journal* (1930), pp.5-7
Victoria County History, *Cambs.* vol.1, (1938) pp.279, 295-6, 300, 313-4
Victoria County History, vol.7, *Cambs.* ii, (1948), pp.15-16, 45
Victoria County History, *Suffolk*, vol.1, (1911) pp.318, 348
Walker, F.G. 'Roman Pottery at Horningsea, Cambs.,' *P.C.A.S.*, vol.17 (1912-13) pp.14-69
Wayne, Joan '*A Foot In Three Daisies,*'   (1987),   pp.64-5
*White's Suffolk Directory*, Sutton, 1885

Documents
Ashmolean Library, Oxford, Rolleston Papers, correspondence
Cambridge University Library, (C.U.L.) Owen, Revd. Add.7652.I/E/74a; Add.7652.I/E/60a., 61, 75; Add.7652II/C/4
Cambridgeshire County Record Office (C.C.R.O.) Bendyshe Papers 14/1; Francis Papers R89/40; P79/8/27 pp.124-6; 65/04;
C.C.R.O. Conybeare Diaries including 22nd March, 28th June1880, 15th December 1881

C.C.R.O. Borough of Camb. Minutes 13th July 1857
Cambridge University Library. MS Plans RA2, Comberton
draft enclosure map 1839-40
Bedfordshire HER, 9415
Cambridgeshire HER  , 00662, 012161, 01776, 02268A,
03216, 03217, 03320/E, 03263, 03438, 04509, 04644, 04692,
04816, 04853, 04978, 04929, 04979, 05032, 050678, 05082,
05129, 05166A, 05186, 05393, 05402, 05546, 06372, 06397,
06495, 06877, 06905, 06928, 08629
Rothamsted Library Archives, A1, Lawes to Henslow 13th
June 1845
Suffolk HER, 03026, 03054, 03851, 03678
Ipswich Museum, card 966-107

Newspapers
Henslow, J.S. Agricultural Gazette, 11th March 1848, p.180
*Cambridge Graphic*, 2nd Nov.1901,p.11
*The Times*, April 16th, 1874


Websites
http://onlinelibrary.wiley.com/doi/10.1002/
ajpa.1330070420/abstract
http://www.badarchaeology.com/wp-content/
uploads/2009/12/foxhall_jaw-300x164.jpg
http://geology.cwru.edu/~huwig/catalog/slides/758.C.1.jpg

www.ingramcontent.com/pod-product-compliance
Lightning Source LLC
Chambersburg PA
CBHW071558270726
48657CB00026B/804